NORFOLK
IN THE
GREAT WAR
A PICTORIAL HISTORY

1914-1918

NEIL R. STOREY

HALSGROVE

Ambulance column passing through St Augustine's, Norwich, c.1915.

Dedication:

This book is for my God Daughter – Liberty
and is dedicated to the memory of all the sons and daughters
of our beloved county who fell or suffered as a result of
The First World War.

First published in Great Britain in 2008

British Library Cataloguing-in-Publication Data.
A CIP record for this title is available from the British Library.

ISBN 978 1 84114 819 9

Halsgrove House
Ryelands Industrial Estate,
Bagley Road, Wellington
Somerset TA21 9PZ
Tel: 01823 653777
Fax: 01823 216796
E-mail: sales@halsgrove.com
Website: www.halsgrove.com

Printed and bound in Great Britain by
CPI Antony Rowe, Chippenham, Wiltshire

Contents

Troops of the 1/1st Nottinghamshire Yeomanry beside their old barn billet in the countryside near Weybourne, November 1914.

Members of a section from 6th (Cyclist) Battalion The Norfolk Regiment enjoy the hospitality of a family on the North Norfolk Coast 1914.

Acknowledgements

My sincere thanks are extended to all who have assisted and encouraged me in my research into the military past of this county over the last twenty years, there are too many to name personally but I wish to record my personal thanks to: Colonel C E Knight MBE, Clare Agate, Clive Wilkins-Jones and the staff of The Norfolk Heritage Centre, Dr John Alban The Norfolk Record Office, BBC Radio Norfolk, Imperial War Museum, Kate Thaxton The Royal Norfolk Regimental Museum, The National Archives, Helen Pugh, Archivist, The British Red Cross Society Archives Department, London, Pamela Willis, Curator of the Order of St John Museum at St John's Gate, London, The Norfolk Family History Society, The Norfolk St John Archive Collection, The Paston School, The Griffon Area Patnership, Dave King, The William Marriott Museum, Swaffham Museum, Major Gary Walker MBE TD RA The Suffolk & Norfolk Yeomanry, Great Yarmouth library, Helen Tovey at *Family Tree Magazine*, University of East Anglia library, Dr Stephen Cherry, Dr Vic Morgan, Peter Stibbons, John Read, James Nice, Ron Clarke, Brian Forman, Janet Steele, Neville Lee, Peter Brooks, Peter Cox, Dick Rayner, Peter Purdy, Peter Smith, Robert 'Bookman' Wright, Elaine Able, Mike Bristow, Les Downham, Simon Butler and all the team at Halsgrove and the late Terry Davy. I also wish to thank my students for their contributions; comments and critique over the years and, of course, my dear family; beloved Molly and son Lawrence for their support and love for this author and his research.

All photographs, pictures and illustrations are from the author's archives unless captioned otherwise.

1 The Road to War

"The past is a foreign country: they do things differently there."
The Go-Between - L P Hartley

At the dawn of the 20th century Norfolk was a county facing a bright and promising future. Although the horse was still the main motive power on the county roads the railways had arrived in the latter half of the 19th century; the networks of the Great Eastern Railway and Midland and Great Northern spanned the county and enabled unprecedented travel and trade opportunities and at a number of locations, what had been sleepy fishing hamlets and coastal towns had blossomed over the last few decades of the 19th century to become fully fledged coastal resorts; Hunstanton, genteel; Great Yarmouth and Gorleston popular with so many, and wonderful Cromer, Sheringham and the surrounding coastline blessed with the evocative magic of Poppyland, so eloquently eulogised by Clement Scott at the zenith of Victorian sentimentality, he caught the imagination of a generation and they came in their

Long dresses and bathing machines, the beach at Cromer in the late 19th century

The heart of Poppyland, The Garden of Sleep, Sidestrand c1914

thousands to walk among those fields of red flowers that swayed and glowed in the sunlight.

The gentry of Norfolk lived an idyllic lifestyle, here were great county families with great country houses and estates that were firm features of the 'seasons' of the peerage and landed. In the county there were well established hunts for fox, hare and stag; here could be found some of the finest game shoots in the country, it was hardly surprising one of the retreats of the Royal family was to be found at Sandringham, so beloved by Edward VII and George V. There was enough coast line for them to find exclusive beaches, indeed Queen Alexandra, wife of Edward VII had a bungalow erected on Snettisham beach in 1908. There were many professionals who made a good living here. Many farmers, business and shop owners had risen to become middle class and also lived well in smart farm, country or town houses, and enjoyed the trappings of wealth; they dressed in fine tailored clothes, had live-in servants, hosted garden parties, organised fetes, often made public displays of benevolence and enjoyed playing prominent roles in their local society.

Dependable and upright, a thoroughly middle-class household at St Cecilia's, Mundesley c1900.

Between 1899 and 1900 The City of Norwich saw its greatest street structure changes since the Norman Conquest with the construction of a tram system to serve both city and suburbs. The big migrations from countryside to city during the 19th century saw the massive expansion of the city population from 36,800 in 1801 to 111,733 in 1901. Up to the 1870s most of these migrants were pouring into the houses already built within the city walls. Originally designed for one family of two parents and four or five children and a couple of servants, as the city population expanded those same houses were soon bought up by landlords and with little or no conversion were leased to perhaps eight families – even utilising the old basements and garrets. Families that had made that move had often suffered dreadful living standards in damp,

cramped, unsanitary, and vermin-infected tenements and filthy courts but many had worked hard and managed to save up to buy – or more likely rent – one of the new terraced houses that had been built beyond the city walls with the accommodation needs of these workers in mind. The rotten tenements still existed in the early 20th century, the worst wards in the city being Ber Street, Coslany and Fye Bridge. Concern for the situation had begun in the mid-19th century; benevolent factory owners like 'the mustard king' Jeremiah James Colman took direct action with their own altruistic gestures of social, educational and health care provision for their large work force. Concerns expressed by leading citizens and the evidence of social surveys pressured the city council to improve the situation and measures to alleviate the plight of the poorest in the city by the improvement of sanitation and by-laws for living conditions were introduced. When City Council-funded female health visitors were also employed, their worth was soon proved, in 1908 alone they made 16,000 visits, in the course of which they found 1222 sick people and gave simple, but very necessary, hygiene advice to the mothers of 2400 infants – undoubtedly with no little thanks to their efforts, increased public awareness of the need for hygiene and the improvement in living conditions in the city between 1899 and 1908 child mortality was reduced from over 180 deaths per thousand births to less than 120.

The Cavalry Barracks at Pockthorpe c1910.

By the early 20th century the City of Norwich was a place of many employment opportunities, not just in the typical city small businesses or high street shops or even the big department stores such as Chamberlin's or Bunting's there were a number of large scale employers such as in the offices of Norwich Union Fire Insurance Society or at three railway stations or in the flour mills, laundries and timber yards; and not forgetting the afore mentioned factories of J.J. Colman at Carrow Works that produced the world famous mustard and a host of other products including starch, corn flour and laundry blue.

Dismounted Lancers from the Cavalry Barracks on the march, a common sight in the city before The Great War.

There were also Harmers Clothing Factory; Caleys who began making mineral water then expanded to manufacture cocoa, chocolate and Christmas crackers and the great breweries of Steward & Patteson, Bullards, Morgans and Youngs, Crawshay & Youngs; the foundries and industry of Barnard, Bishop and Barnard (Charles Barnard built the world's first wire-netting machine in 1844), Laurence and Scott and Boulton & Paul. But above all Norwich was a centre of shoe manufacture with the massive 'super factories' of Howlett & White, Sexton & Everards, James Southall & Co. and Edwards & Holmes dominating the scene there were also a number of smaller firms which in total employed nearly 8,000 citizens in the shoe trade alone.

In a city of so many jobs there were still those who could not find work. To support those in need there was the Norwich Distress Committee who could pay a 'dole.' Surprisingly in a city of over 100,000 the applications for dole received by the committee in 1908-9 numbered 2734. Families who had not managed to make a go of it or dared to take up the challenge of a new start in a 'land of opportunity' could seek help from the Norwich Distress Committee who would put up posters appealing for unskilled labourers, navvies, domestic servants and all willing workers to go (with the assistance of the committee) to 'Canada: Britain's nearest and greatest colony.' If you were a tenant farmer you could also be tempted by offers of 160 acres free to the man and his family who sought a new start in the New World. Under a variety of local and national initiatives hundreds of families from the city and county with children aged upwards of 11 months were sent or given assisted passage from Norfolk to Canada, Australia and New Zealand. This was, however, an expensive venture for example, to send a party of 53 men, women and children from Norwich to Toronto in 1906 cost over £400.

Agriculture was still the largest source of employment across the county and the working conditions for the agricultural labourer were improving after George Edwards founded the Eastern Counties Agricultural Labourers & Small Holders Union (later known as the National Union of Agricultural and Allied Workers) at North Walsham in 1906, and became its general secretary. However, it was still a bit 'tight' in the winter time when there was very little work to be had on the land so with so many men turned their hand to whatever they could to tide them over until spring sowing, some even walked to 'go on the boats' and sailed as hands on the fishing trawlers out of Great Yarmouth. Those who had managed to earn a living in the country worked hard, from sun up to sun down, but they too often suffered a life living in sub-standard cottages – very charming and 'rustic' to look at in old photographs but often draughty, damp and leaky, especially if there was a hole in the thatch above *your* bed.

Britannia Barracks, Depot of The Norfolk Regiment c1910.

Such was the background of so many Norfolk men. To escape the often hand to mouth experience of living and working in the country or to escape the tenements of the city, to seek adventure and see the world many young, fit men from our county walked up the hill to Mousehold, through the gates of Britannia Barracks and joined the colours with the Regular Army battalions of The Norfolk Regiment.

A modern historian must always be mindful of the danger of the accounts from those who look back on the past with rose-tinted spectacles but temper that with a strong sense of empathy. However, even couched in those terms there does appear to have been far closer extended family ties in the early 20th century than we generally know today; perhaps such ties were inevitable when in many cases the extended family of Grandparents, Mother, Father and children shared the same roof, contributed to the same pot and shared their trials and tribulations as a family seeing unity as strength. Or perhaps it was the shared fight to keep the family fed, or out of the workhouse or together in the face of domestic violence or a parent who spend the family money down the pub (or both). Often it only took an injury, sickness or death of one parent to send a family into a tragic downward spiral to destitution. Tragically some of the social evils we know today were just the same and far worse in the hard-up streets of the past.

Some of the children left destitute and alone by family or fate found a new start in Norfolk. The old Norfolk County School set up in the 1870s to serve the

The marching band of The Watt's Naval Training College c1906.

educational needs of the 'sons of farmers and artisans' was turned into a home for orphans and destitute boys under the auspices of Dr Thomas Barnardo in March 1903. The cost of furnishing the institution for 300 boys and the necessary staff was covered by Fenwick S Watts Esq. in memory of his father. Formally opened by the Earl of Leicester on 17 April 1906. The school maintained the name of its last owner – Watt's Naval Training College and was used for the training of selected

Admiral of the Fleet, Sir Arthur Knyvet Wilson VC, GCB, OM, GCVO.

Admiral of the Fleet John "Jackie" Fisher, 1st Baron Fisher of Kilverstone.

Barnardo's boys for a life at sea in the Royal Navy or Mercantile Marine. Orphan and destitute boys between 11 and 14 years of age were admitted for a two year course of general education followed, upon attaining the age of 14, by a two year course of Naval Training. Most of these lads then progressed to Royal Naval Training Establishment HMS *Ganges*, at Shotley, Suffolk.

The Watt's boys followed a long tradition of Norfolk men making fine sea farers, be they hardy fishermen, brave sailors, gallant lifeboatmen or heroes like Admiral Nelson of Burnham Thorpe and Admiral Sir Arthur Knyvet 'Tug' Wilson VC of Swaffham. Wilson had earned his VC while serving as Captain of HMS *Hecla* on 29 February 1884 during the British Sudan Campaign. The Naval brigade was making a landing at El Teb, upon hearing of an officer (Lieutenant Royds RN) being mortally wounded he attached himself to a gun battery and went forward on the right hand side of the advance. As the troops closed on the enemy's Krupp battery the Arabs charged out on the corner of the square and on the Royal Navy detachment who were dragging the Gardner gun. The men were vulnerable and they could easily have been over-run. Captain Wilson knew instinctively that they would have to fight or die, any lack of zeal, any falter and all would be lost; he sprang to the front and engaged in single combat with some of the enemy with his sword, but in the process the blade was broken from its hilt and disappeared into the sand leaving Wilson with nothing more than a glorified knuckle duster, but fight on he did, thus protecting this detachment till some men of the York and Lancaster Regiment came to his assistance with their bayonets.

Wilson's citation concludes 'But for the action of this Officer, Sir Redvers Buller thinks that one or more of his detachment must have been speared. Captain Wilson was wounded but remained with the battery during the day.'

A career Naval Officer, Wilson rose through the ranks to the rank of Admiral of the Fleet and made a significant contribution to the Royal Navy as a whole through his own innovations and support for the development of new weaponry for modern naval warfare notably in torpedoes and submarines. Wilson was also a staunch supporter of Admiral Sir John 'Jackie' Fisher of Kilverston Hall when Fisher was First Sea Lord and with Fisher was a leading voice in the 'old guard push' to persuade all concerned the investment would be worthwhile for HMS *Dreadnought* – the first all iron clad, all big gun, turbine driven battleship which truly led to Britannia ruling the waves!

HMS Dreadnought *and the British Fleet off Gorleston 1906.*

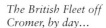

*The British Fleet off
Cromer, by day...*

... and by night!

The revolutionary HMS *Dreadnought* entered service in 1906. *Dreadnought* represented such a marked advance in naval technology that all other existing battleships were rendered obsolete, her name came to be associated with an entire generation of battleships – the 'Dreadnoughts' and henceforward all surface navies would be measured by their Dreadnought strength. Kaiser Wilhelm II nurtured a desire to construct a German navy capable of challenging the maritime dominance of the Royal Navy and entrusted the expansion of the German Navy to his Naval minister and close adviser Admiral Alfred von Tirpitz. Tirpitz expanded the German Navy by championing four Fleet Acts between 1898 and 1912 and in the wake of Dreadnought set about building Germany's own version of the new generation of battleships. Thus began a Navy race that was to become an aggressive thorn in the side of Anglo-German relations, particularly threatening British pre-eminence in colonial and trade spheres and, ultimately, a major contributing factor to the outbreak of war in 1914.

The children who were maturing to man and womanhood in the early 20th century, had been a generation that had benefitted from the 1870 Foster Education Act and having been schooled in the three 'R's of Reading, wRiting and aRithemtic. They could look to a greater variety of employment opportunities than any generation before. Cross country transport and international

*The Masters and boys of
Tenison House at The
Paston School c1914.*

shipping could mean the world, or at least the great British Empire was their oyster. But these children were different; they had not only been schooled in education, they had been educated in patriotism. Schools would often have flag poles and begin and end each day with a flag ceremony, the children would give thanks to the monarch in their prayers and with the empire at its zenith the children's text books and lessons would regularly include overt and subtle references to it. Childrens' illustrated story papers such as *The Boy's Own Paper* and *Union Jack* were filled with tales of brave and patriotic young folk and school prize books hammered home this ethos with volumes swathed in suitably dramatic pictorial covers that told stories of derring do from English history and the exploits of the men who built and fought to defend the far flung outposts of the British Empire by such authors as G A Henty, Captain F S Brereton and Rudyard Kipling.

From 1902 there was even Empire Day every 24 May (held on the birthday of the late Queen and Empress); an event consisting of costumed parades, speeches and much flag waving in both the physical and metaphorical sense was created with the express intention to 'remind children that they formed part of the British Empire, and that they might think with others in lands across the sea, what it meant to be sons and daughters of such a glorious Empire (and to reinforce) The strength of the Empire depended upon them, and they must never forget it.' Patriotism, sense of duty and loyalty to the monarch pervaded every child's education.

The greater affluence of the new middle class in the 19th century also saw the unprecedented expansion and creation of Grammar Schools and new public schools. Above all the public schools were the heartlands of the new generation of young men being prepared through education and tutored to aspire to lead as managers, business directors and captains of industry and above all a new generation of ultra patriotic military leaders fit to be Officers *and* gentlemen. The vision of these schools as seed beds of future officers was capitalised on by Richard Burdon Haldane (Secretary of State for War 1905 to 1912), his dramatic reformation of the British Army saw a brand new approach to the methods of military operations and standardised training; the creation of a British Expeditionary Force and a complete overhaul of the old Volunteer system to create a modern Territorial Force; but first of all he created the Officers Training Corps in 1907. The movement had two divisions: 'Senior' based in the

George Howson, headmaster, (seated centre) and the Masters of Gresham's School c1905.

Universities and 'Junior' working in the schools but both working with the express aim of providing as many officers as possible for the Special Reserve and the new Territorial Force.

It is hardly surprising that Gresham's School at Holt embraced the Officers Training Corps wholeheartedly, indeed, membership of the OTC was soon compulsory at the school. Their instructor in carpentry was ex-Quartermaster Sergeant Davies late of the Royal Horse Artillery and the formidable ex-Colour-Sergeant Instructor Steer, late Scots Guards, who led the boys in drill, swimming and gymnastics – it was remarked in the school magazine: 'No one who was here when he first arrived will ever forget the way he electrified the Corps by his smartness. It was a familiar saying in those days that his salute could be heard.' With a ready pool of expertise and some keen masters; Captain John Chambré Miller the Master of Modern Languages and Captain W. Foster Bushell MA (Assistant Master) two infantry companies of the OTC Junior Division were raised and the boys learned drill and skill-at-arms with alacrity. A band was also mustered to smartly lead the boys on parade and soon they were off on manoeuvres across the school field and surrounding heath land camping and attending central OTC camps with other schools. Haldane's vision matured in 1914 and in the first seven months of the war, the OTC provided over 20,000 commissioned officers – many of them joining their regiments straight from school.

The greatest task implemented by Haldane was to be the complete reorganisation of the Home Field Army and Reserve System, which created the

The 1st Norfolk Royal Garrison Artillery marching out of Harleston for manoeuvres c1905.

Territorial Force from the old Volunteer System and the provision of the British Expeditionary Force. The notion being that the regular battalions would provide the garrison troops for the Empire and form a BEF from 'Home' garrisoned troops in the event of a 'war emergency' while it was intended that the Territorial Force should remain at home and defend Britain.

In 1907 there were 221 battalions of volunteer infantry in England, Scotland and Wales. The new scheme saw line infantry regiment battalions given sequential numbers ie; The Regular Battalions were the 1st and 2nd, the 3rd became a Militia Battalion and the Territorials 4th and 5th Battalions. Under the Haldane Reforms, officially introduced on 1 April 1908, The Norfolk Regiment was allocated three Battalions in the new Territorial Force. These new battalions were initially created out of the old Norfolk Volunteers; the 4th Battalion drawing its men from the 1st and 2nd V.B.s and the 5th Battalion from the 3rd and 4th V.B.s respectively. The Norfolk Regiment was also granted the honour of raising one of the much heralded eleven Cyclist Battalions (Eight English, two Scottish and one Welsh) included in the scheme thus our final Battalion was designated 6th Battalion (Cyclists) T. F.

E (Sandringham) Company, 3rd Volunteer Battalion, The Norfolk Regiment leaving for one of the last volunteers summer camps at Aldershot from Wolferton Station, July 1906.

The new Norfolk Territorial Battalions were made up of eight companies, each of which consisted of about 4 officers and a hundred men. Although a few came from outside, most of them were Norfolk men and just about all parts of the county were represented. The allocation of men to each company depended largely upon in which part of the county they lived or worked. This suited most recruits who were more than happy to serve with their relations, friends and acquaintances and it made the battalion a close knit society. In fact amongst all ranks the battalion was riddled with complicated family ties of uncles, nephews, brothers and cousins serving side by side and throughout the various companies. Its rank structure reflected society at the time: the officers were from the local gentry or the directors of larger local industries, the NCOs works foremen and ex-servicemen and the Other Ranks comprised of domestic staff, labourers, gardeners and estate workers.

The visit of HM King Edward VII to Norwich on 25 October 1909 was the first major gathering of the Norfolk Territorials at a grand review on Mousehold

HM King Edward VII outside the Chapelfield Drill Hall on his official visit to Norwich 25 October 1909.

Heath. On the day 11,000 city children were marshalled onto the heath in front of Britannia Barracks to sing to the King and thousands more came to wave flags and watch the spectacle. Over 3000 troops were on parade including Yeomanry, Artillery, Infantry, Cyclists, Army Service and Medical Corps under the overall command of Brigadier General J H Campbell, the commander of the East Anglian Division. Lining parties and a parade contingent were also provided by the members of the Royal Norfolk Veterans Association. The RNVA (founded 1898) was one of the very first ex-serviceman's welfare associations in the country and comprised Norfolk men who had served in The Royal Navy and many various branches and regiments of the British Army in campaigns going back to the 1840s. Their smart turnout, polished boots and fine array of bright medal ribbons and shiny medals are remembered by all who saw this parade and later a bronze medal was struck by the veterans to commemorate the occasion. But the highlight of the occasion for the military was the presentation of colours by the King to the KORR Norfolk Yeomanry, the 4th and 5th Territorial Battalions of The Norfolk Regiment. This magnificent occasion was concluded with a general march past by all units. The King then retired for luncheon at the Officer's Mess at the Chapel Field Drill Hall. The whole event was one of the earliest occasions in Norwich to be captured on moving film.

In 1912 British Army manoeuvres of an unprecedented scale in Great Britain were conducted across East Anglia. They almost did not take place at all after

Left: *The black draped drums of G Company 5th Battalion, The Norfolk Regiment at the memorial parade for the late King Edward VII, Great Yarmouth 1910.*

Right: *Royal Navy Reservists and the troops of the Yarmouth Battery (late Prince of Wales Own Norfolk Artillery Militia) at the memorial parade for Edward VII.*

The Guards marching out of Swaffham Market Place during the 'Great Manoeuvres' 1912.

torrential rain fall caused extensive flooding and drowned a number of camps that had been set up prior to commencement, indeed the special correspondent despatched by *The Times*, recorded 'As I stand by the side of a Norfolk turnpike, this inimitable infantry swung by, wet to the skin, perhaps chilled to the marrow, chanting a roundelay to prove it takes more than weather to fathom the bottom of the *esprit* of British infantry,' almost a premonition of phrases to appear again in 1914 and 1939.

Men of 2nd Battalion, Coldstream Guards with manoeuvre bands on their hats marching out to do battle across the South Norfolk countryside during the 'Great Manoeuvres' 1912.

On 12 September the correspondent wrote 'Today, thank goodness, a change has come. The bitter north wind has dropped, the mists have rolled away off the Norfolk Broads and the kindly sun has dried the wringing khaki of the gallant men who were moved yesterday into standing camp to relieve them of the rigours of the cheerless bivouac. With the weather improved the manoeuvres went ahead as planned. The general idea of the exercise was that the coast line of East Anglia represented the frontier between an imaginary Red enemy under the command of Lieut General Sir Douglas Haig and Blue England commanded by Lieutenant General Sir James Grierson. The Red army had crossed the frontier between Wells and Hunstanton and was moving southward when operations began. Blue had ordered a general mobilization and was urgent to prevent the entry of Red troops into London. In order to confine troops within reasonable limits an area of ten miles broad was declared as 'impassable' from the Wash to Somersham. Each force consisted of a cavalry division, two infantry divisions, army troops, two aeroplane flights and each side also had an airship (The airships were named *Gamma* and *Delta*). To monitor and referee the manoeuvres the Chief Umpire was General Sir John French, and with his Staff he based himself in Cambridge, he was later joined by The King and other international military dignitaries and delegations.

The forces were nearly equal in size. The Staff of the Red Army were Aldershot command, who were accustomed to working together. In contrast, the Blue Staff were drawn from all commands except Aldershot. Red cavalry and infantry were all regular Aldershot divisions. Conversely the Blue had two brigades drawn from Household Cavalry, Scots Greys, Yeomanry and Cyclists and the Blue infantry came from the Southern Command (3rd Division) and Eastern Command (4th Division) and Territorial Force. The main concentration of troops in Norfolk was in Swaffham with over 2000 'Red' troops predominantly from 2nd and 3rd Grenadier Guards and 2nd Coldstream Guards. All ranks and services included, the total number of troops involved across East Anglia amounted to nearly 50,000.

The public had already had their appetites whetted during the Aldershot Command Training before the commencement of the main manoeuvres. The special correspondent from *The Times* had been sent to Thetford and sent his report dramatically headlined: 'A Battle at Dawn', it concludes 'The Aldershot Army has become a flank guard and has already had a brush with the advance guard of the Swaffham enemy. The menace from this direction is so great that the second army has detached a brigade of infantry to help the flank guard. At sundown the river Wissey, a tributary of the Ouse, separated the outposts of the opposing forces, and early tomorrow an issue of great importance will be decided. The announcement here that Sir Douglas Haig's army is marching by night to the drifts will disclose nothing to the enemy, as by the time this despatch is public, the battle will be lost and won.'

On the eve before the main manoeuvres the Red cavalry was at Barnham and Euston with patrols on the line of the river Lark as far south as Bury St Edmunds. The rest of the Red army was halted for the night in the areas of Stoke Ferry, Methwold, Mundford, Sandford, Watton and Swaffham with Red communications running through Wells with an advance base at East Dereham. At 6am on 16 September 1912, it was declared 'commencement of hostilities' and both sides went into action knowing time was critical to success of failure. Both local and national papers avidly followed the manoeuvres and public interest grew apace with each 'action' particularly if they recognised somewhere in their locality.

And still more marched on, the locals had never seen anything like it.

Many country folks stood on the streets and by the fields and watched in amazement; many had undoubtedly seen the local volunteers or the new Territorials on their weekend manoeuvres or Field Days but they really had never seen anything on this scale before. It was the last of the gentlemanly experience of warfare, yes lessons had been learned since the Boer war, kit and weaponry had evolved but still the senior officers rode their horses in front of their men and marker flags were carried to show the progress of the advancing troops in action. Such flags were to play a fateful role in the battles of the Great War when it came and the fate of many a young soldier could depend on whether some report, accurate or not, had been received of marker flags being seen in enemy trenches during an attack.

Grenadier Guards resting in Swaffham Market place during the 'Great Manoeuves' 1912.

During the manoeuvres it soon became abundantly clear Haig had not realised the importance of the spotter aircraft. Grierson, the victor, had hidden his troops from observation and Haig had failed to ascertain the movements or deployment of the Blue forces. In contrast, Grierson had almost perfect knowledge of the movements of Haig's troops. In the final analysis of the manoeuvres in spite of the efforts of the umpires and judges to make the contest appear more even, Haig was simply out-generalled by Grierson.

In 1912 the new Territorial Force had comfortably established itself in Norfolk. The last of this first batch of new units in the county had been the 'Carrow Territorials' who proudly announced in the J &J Colman in-house *Carrow Works Magazine* that they would provide a section of Territorial Artillery attached to 3rd Norfolk Battery, East Anglian Brigade, Royal Field Artillery. This half battery had its home in the old Carrow Ice House which was able to accommodate two field guns, limbers and associated harness and equipment for the horses to pull them. An area of ground in front of the Ice House was given over to gun drill and battery manoeuvres while the gymnasium was put at their disposal for personal training and drill in wet weather. By the time the magazine had gone to press (July 1912) the battery had spent Whitsuntide under canvas for a training camp. Under the command of Lieutenant R H Lane (of the Carrow Works Counting House Staff) they had mounted parades, gun drills, lectures and even a church parade at St John de Sepulchre Church on Sunday. In the 'By the Way' page of the same magazine comment was made 'We venture to express the fervent hope that whatever

Left: The 'Carrow Works Section', 3rd Norfolk Battery, East Anglian Brigade, Royal Field Artillery, 1912.

Right: Officers from 1st East Anglian Brigade Royal Field Artillery on weekend camp at Crown Point, near Norwich 1909.

Horse lines of 1st East Anglian Brigade Royal Field Artillery on weekend camp at Crown Point, near Norwich 1909.

laurels may fall to the lot of the Carrow section of the 3rd Norfolk Battery will be won on the parade ground and not on the field of battle.'

The year 1912 also saw the first full public publication of the newly structured military units of the county in *Kelly's Directory of Norfolk* and with very few amendments the following land forces formations were those mobilized from the county on the outbreak of war in 1914.

Norfolk was part of Eastern Command and formed part of the No. 9 Grouped Regimental District which had its headquarters at Warley in Essex. Britannia Barracks in Norwich was the Regimental Depot for the 1st and 2nd Regular Battalions and 3rd Special Reserve Battalion of The Norfolk Regiment. Also in the city were the Cavalry Barracks occupied by XIIth (Prince of Wales's) Royal Lancers and the local Divisional Offices of Royal Engineers under Capt E J Bone and Army Service Corps Commanded by Capt W H Barton at 11 Britannia Road

Other Regular Army troops in the county The No. 4 Depot of the Royal Garrison Artillery had its headquarters on the South Denes, Great Yarmouth under the Command of Major R H M McCulloch DSO with Second in Command Captain G. Badham Thornhill and Lieut. G. C. Spinks as District Officer. At the same barracks were a detachment of Royal Army Medical Corps under Major C W Allport MD.

The Norfolk Territorial Force comprised the following units:

The King's Own Royal Regiment Norfolk Yeomanry (Eastern Mounted Brigade)

 Headquarters: Cattle Market Street, Norwich.

 Staff: Commanding Lieut-Col. Henry Albert Barclay CVO ADC; Adjutant Capt. The Hon. R N D Ryder (8th Hussars); Quartermaster Hon. Lieut. J. A. Sayer; Medical Officer, Surgeon-Major J F Gordon-Dill; Chaplain Rev F A S ffolkes MVO BA (TF) Regimental Sergeant-Major George Hugdell

 A Squadron: Major A R Buxton; Second-in-Command Captain G T Bullard; Squadron Sergeant-Major E. Broadley (Cattle Market Street, Norwich)

 B Squadron: Major A F Morse; Second-in-Command Capt J F Barclay; Squadron Sergeant-Major T. Elliott (Grammar School Road, North Walsham)

Lieut-Col. Henry Albert Barclay CVO ADC, Commanding Officer of The King's Own Royal Regiment Norfolk Yeomanry.

Members of The Norfolk Yeomanry at camp 1912.

C Squadron: Major C D Seymour; Second-in-Command Capt Lord Hastings, Squadron Sergt-Major William Stonehouse (Holt Road, Fakenham)

D Squadron: Major C F Gurney; Second-in-Command Lieut H A Birkbeck; Squadron Sergeant Major G. Jolly (Gaywood Road, King's Lynn)

1st East Anglian Brigade, Royal Field Artillery (3 Batteries)

Headquarters: Old Militia Barracks, All Saints Green, Norwich

Staff: Commanding Lt Col R E A Le Mottée RA; Adjutant Capt D H K Hunter; Medical Officer Capt J C R Robinson RAMC (TF)

1st Norfolk Battery: Major Percy Wiltshire; Drill Instructor Battery Sergt-Major Aaron Joseph Lawson (Nelson Road, Great Yarmouth)

2nd Norfolk Battery: Major Gilbert Willian Daynes, Drill Instructor Battery Sergt-Major James Bourne (All Saints Green, Norwich)

3rd Norfolk Battery: Major S G Allen, Drill Instructor Battery Sergt-Major J H Hannant (All Saints Green, Norwich)

1st East Anglian Ammunition Column: Drill Instructor Sergt-Major J. Hughes (All Saints Green, Norwich)

The Norfolk & Suffolk Infantry Brigade comprised the Territorial Battalions of the Norfolk and Suffolk Regiments and had its headquarters at 18a Prince of Wales Road.

The drums of 4th Battalion, The Norfolk Regiment at the Chapel Field Drill Hall, shortly after their parade on the occasion of King Edward VII's visit to Norwich, 25 October 1909.

4th Battalion, The Norfolk Regiment (TF)

Honourary Colonel: The Earl of Leicester CMG, GCVO (Lord Lieutenant)

Headquarters: Drill Hall Chapel Field, Norwich.

Staff: Commanding Lt-Col J R Harvey DSO; Majors E. Mornement TD and F G W Wood; Instructor of Musketry Capt W H M Andrews; Adjutant Capt F R Day (Norfolk Regt.), Quarter-Master Hon. Lieut. R W Moore; Medical Officer Lieut. J H Owens RAMC (TF); Chaplains Rev E W Hardy and Rev. C. U. Manning.

A Company: Capt S D Page (Chapel Field Road, Norwich)

B Company: Capt W H M Andrews (Chapel Field Road, Norwich)

C Company: Capt H R Rudd (Chapel Field Road, Norwich)

Colour-Sergt. Instructor C E Medlicott and Sergt.-Major Hemmings, Drill Instructors

D Company: Lieut S H W Coxon (Denmark Street, Diss) Sergt. Thomas Stubbs, Drill Instructor

E Company: Capt Herbert Charles Long (Attleborough with Detachments at East Harling and Hingham)

Colour-Sergt. Instructor J. Munnings

F Company: Capt. Henry R. Fletcher (Drill Hall, Town Green, Wymondham) Sergt.-Instructor Alfred Pitcher, Drill Instructor

G Company: Capt H E Holmes (Guildhall, Thetford and Brandon) Capt. C W W Burrell Colour-Sergt. James William Hall, Drill Instructor

H Company: Capt R T E Gilbert (Thorpe St Andrew)

Some of the boys from F Company, 5th Battalion, The Norfolk Regiment off to Territorial camp, from Sheringham Station, July 1910.

5th Battalion, The Norfolk Regiment (TF)

Honourary Colonel: The Earl of Albemarle CB, KCVO, JP, DL, VD

Headquarters: Quebec Street, East Dereham.

Staff: Commanding Lt.-Col P J Petrie; Second in Command Lt-Col & Hon Colonel T P Angell VD; Major A W Thomas VD; Instructor of Musketry Lieut E R Cubitt; Adjutant Capt. A E M Ward (Norfolk Regiment); Quarter Master Hon. Major A. Smith VD; Chaplain Rev. A R H Grant

A Company: Capt Edward Milligen Beloe (Nelson Street, King's Lynn)

Sergt.-Instructor Henry Harwood

B Company: Lieut S A Coxon (Downham)

Sergt.-Major W. Ford, Drill Instructor

C Company: Capt Herbert Ellis Rowell (Holt Road, Fakenham and Crown Hotel, Wells Detachment)
Colour-Sergeant Frank Harris, Drill Instructor
Capt Thomas Woods Purdy (Pound Road, Aylsham Detachment)
Sergt.-Instructor Thomas Davis

D Company: Capt Walter John Barton (Quebec Street, East Dereham and Castleacre Street, Swaffham Detachment)
Sergt.-Instructor W H Adcock (East Dereham)
Colour-Sergt. Charles Brewster, Instructor (Swaffham Detachment)

E Company: Capt Frank Reginald Beck MVO (Sandringham)

F Company: Capt Havard Noel Bridgwater (Central Road Cromer with Detachments at Sheringham, Holt and Melton Constable)
Sergt.-Instructor Samuel Parker, Drill Instructor (Cromer)
Colour-Sergt.-Instructor Hall, Drill Instructor (Holt Detachment)

G Company: Capt Leonard Joynson Brown (York Road, Great Yarmouth)
Lieut W L Blake

H Company: Capt T B Hall (York Road, Great Yarmouth)
Colour-Sergt. H. White, Drill Instructor
Lieut. E R Cubitt (North Walsham Detachment)
Sergt. J. Coe, Drill Instructor

6th Battalion, The Norfolk Regiment (TF)

Honourary Colonel: Colonel Henry Tyrwhitt Staniforth Patteson JP DL VD

Headquarters: Cattle Market Street, Norwich.

Staff: Commanding Lt.-Col Bernard Henry Leathes Prior; Second in Command: Major Frank Sidney Ayre; Adjutant Capt. F Higson (Norfolk Regiment); Quarter Master Hon. Major H. Moss; Chaplain Rev. G F Packer

Sergt Major Charles H Vincent
Quarter-Master Sergeant H W Horsley

6th (Cyclist) Battalion, The Norfolk Regiment on parade at summer training camp, Boughton Park, Kettering, September 1913.

Sergt Bugler C L Potter
Cook Sergeant R A Smith
Transport Sergt. G Crane
Communication Section:

Capt O H Cockrill (Great Yarmouth)

Signalling Sergeant G C Baird (Great Yarmouth)

Motor Cycle Sergt. D. Jenner (Fakenham)

Machine Gun Section
Sergt C T Ransome

A Company: Capt W E Salter (Cattle Market Street, Norwich)
2nd Lieut G.W. Köblich
Colour-Sergt F E Smith

B Company (Drill Hall, York Road, Great Yarmouth)
Capt S R Woodger
2nd Lieut G W Miles
Colour-Sergt. G D Gibbons
Colour-Sergt. Instructor H. Richardson

C Company (King's Lynn with Detachments at Terrington and Tilney)
Lieut A E Coulton
2nd Lieut H. Le P. Grimwade
Colour-Sergt. D Melton
Colour-Sergt. Instructor F Henderson

D Company (Station Road, Thetford with a Detachment at Attleborough)
Lieut M A Trotter
Colour-Sergt J. Marshall
Colour-Sergt. William James White, Instructor

E Company (Holt Road, Fakenham)
Capt. Sidney Dewing
Colour-Sergt. A Bird
Colour-Sergt. Instructor Edmund Scotchmer

F Company (Ditchingham)
Lieut. C. Peek Philpott
Colour-Sergt. F. Morriss
Colour-Sergt. Instructor A. Hall

G Company (Watton & Swaffham)
Lieut G W Barnham
Colour-Sergt J L Heyhoe
Colour-Sergt. H. Lynn Drill Instructor

H Company (Norwich)
Capt. S T Tunbridge
Colour-Sergt. W F Clabburn

East Anglian Division (Norfolk & Suffolk Brigade Company) Army Service Corps

Transport & Supply Column

Headquarters: Tuesday Market Street, King's Lynn

Commanding: Captain E R Hawkins

Sergt-Major Instructor C. Holloway

*Wagon and team
belonging to the East
Anglian Division
(Norfolk & Suffolk
Brigade Company)
A.S.C. Transport &
Supply Column,
King's Lynn c1913.*

2nd East Anglian Field Ambulance, Royal Army Medical Corps

   Headquarters: Bethel Street, Norwich

   Staff: Commanding: Lieut-Col. J H Stacy; Major G B Masson; Capt J M G
      Bremner

   Quartermaster: Hon. Lieut. R. S. Mason, Transport Officer: Hon. Lieut. E J
      Edwards

   Chaplain: Rev. J C Titcombe (TF): Instructor: Sergt-Major James Connell

It is not without some significance that in the 1912 *Kelly's Directory* the county
organisation of the Boy Scout movement (founded by Boer War hero Robert
Baden Powell in 1907) that epitomised and espoused the ideals for patriotic and
dutiful boys is listed directly under the military forces of the county. During this
period the patriotic ethos was omnipotent in public life and a number of local

*Boy Scouts on parade in
Norwich Cathedral
Close, Coronation Day
22 June 1911.*

A fine display by the boys of Norwich Sea Cadet Corps. In 1912 aboard their training brig Lord Nelson *c1912.*

cadet corps were also created. In 1911 one of the first achievements of the newly formed Norfolk and Norwich Branch of the Navy League was the creation of the Norwich Sea Cadet Corps. In 1912 a subscription raised the necessary money to buy the old Lowestoft trawler *Elsie* and fit her out as a training brig renamed *Lord Nelson.* The Cadet Norfolk Artillery was also formed in 1911, received official recognition in April 1913 and was affiliated to 1st East Anglian Brigade Royal Field Artillery (TF).

The last peacetime showcase for the Territorial Force in Norfolk came in July 1914 when the Norfolk and Suffolk Brigade held their two week camp on the Holkham Estate. The Brigade on this camp comprised the 4th and 5th Battalions Norfolk Regiment, 5th Suffolks, 2nd East Anglian Brigade Royal Army Medical Corps (T.F.), Norfolk and Suffolk Company of the Army Service Corps (T.F.). During the week they worked together in field operations and played in sporting competitions in the evenings. The culmination of the camp was a parade of over 2000 Territorials, marching past in extended column of companies with colours flying and bayonets fixed, the Earl of Leicester, Lord Lieutenant of Norfolk joined by Major General E S Inglefield CB DSO, the General Officer Commanding the East Anglian Division. Once the parade had marched past, the troops formed a square and were addressed by the Lord Lieutenant who expressed his great pleasure at what he had seen, not only on parade but throughout the week's camp stating 'You marched past well and if each battalion is called upon for more serious work it will do its duty to uphold the honour of its county and country.' For many men it would seem like were never out of khaki again because they found OHMS envelopes warning of the embodiment of the Territorial Force waiting for them when they returned home.

The last great parade of the The Norfolk & Suffolk Brigade of the Territorial Force. Over 2000 Territorials march past the Earl of Leicester, President of the County Territorial Association and Major General E S Inglefield CB DSO, the General Officer Commanding the East Anglian Division at Holkham, July 1914.

2 Outbreak and Mobilization for War 1914

In the early days of August 1914 it was not a question of if there was going to be war with Germany, but when. The permanent staff of the Norfolk & Suffolk Territorial Infantry Brigade had set up an office in the Royal Hotel at Great Yarmouth and the Brigadier and his staff proceeded there immediately after the Holkham Camp and the adjutants of the various companies made arrangements to place themselves in close contact with their respective headquarters and keeping a weather eye on the post offices who had extended the hours of their telegraph service in the event of urgent announcements or orders being transmitted.

With Europe edging ever closer to the precipice of war it was time to take a holiday while one could, the weather was excellent and the coastal resorts were enjoying a bumper season. Clementine Churchill took the children for a bucket-and-spade holiday on the Norfolk coast. They stayed at Pear Tree Cottage at Overstrand, near Cromer. While still working unrelentingly to bring the Royal Navy up to the highest state of readiness for war, Winston joined them at weekends and would mobilize all the children on the beach to build giant sandcastles and man their defences against the incoming sea.

In the last days of July, Winston, abandoning his family by the seaside, hurried back to London to postpone the dispersal of the First and Second Fleets and the demobilization of the Third – an act initiated after a phone call from the nearby Sea Marge Hotel (there was no telephone at Pear Tree Cottage). By the end of the month he was able to report to the King:

31 July 1914
Admiralty
12.30 a.m.
Secret

Sir,

Your Majesty is informed of the diplomatic, so I confine myself to the military aspect.

The First Fleet is now in the open seas. The Second Fleet will assemble tomorrow at Portland. All 'precautionary' measures have (so

Left: *Gee's Troubadours who played at Yarmouth during the summer season 1914.*

Middle: *Catlin's Royal Pierrots played Britannia Pier, Great Yarmouth 1914.*

Right: *Henry Clay's Musical Party played Gorleston Pavilion and Bandstand 1914.*

far) behaved magnificently. The four old battleships will reach the Humber tomorrow. All the flotillas have reached their stations ...

The following night, acting on his own responsibility, Churchill instigated the summons to all Reservists for the full mobilization of the Fleet. He wrote to his 'Clemmie' at Cromer:

Secret
Not to be left about but locked up or burned
    My darling,
    There is still hope although the clouds are blacker & blacker. Germany is realising I think how great are the forces against her & is trying tardily to restrain her idiot ally. We are working to soothe Russia. But everybody is preparing swiftly for war. And at any moment now the stroke may fall. We are ready...

Two days later Germany declared war on Russia and on 3 August her forces invaded Belgium. Britain's ultimatum to Germany, demanding respect for Belgian neutrality, expired at midnight (German time) the following night. At that instant Churchill flashed the fateful signal to all HM Ships and Naval Establishments:

4 August 1914
Admiralty
11 p.m.
COMMENCE HOSTILITIES AGAINST GERMANY

In *Twenty-One Years* Randolph Churchill recorded his memories, as a boy of three, of the coming of the war:

We were staying at the seaside ... There was a lot of excitement and my father had to go to London. One day we were told that war had come. We looked out to sea expecting that German ships would soon come into view but nothing happened, except that my father could not come down from London. We children were all disappointed — no Germans and no Papa.

In the county of Norfolk, over the weekend of 1 and 2 August 1914 a palpable military presence manifested as soldiers were posted to guard key areas such as railway stations, utilities, wireless stations and military installations such as the Yarmouth Coastguard Station which had been taken over as the headquarters of the Flying Corps Staff. The people of the nation and the county knew they were on the brink of war. First to be called were the men of the Royal Naval Reserve, most of whom lived in the towns and hamlets along the coast. The Admiralty order calling up all classes of naval reserves reached some towns as early as 4 o'clock on the morning of Sunday 2 August. In *Norwich War Record* (1920), Herbert Leeds recalled the day, 'Motor cars sped into the neighbouring villages, and a cutter went down into The Wash carrying instructions to those who were with the fishing fleet. There were about sixty Naval Reservists in King's Lynn, and by one o'clock forty-eight out of the sixty presented themselves in uniform at Lynn Custom House. They left by train in the

*The mobilized Royal
Navy Reservists draw
quite a crowd in front of
the King's Lynn Custom
House, 2 August 1914.*

afternoon for Chatham and were given an enthusiastic send off.' At Great Yarmouth the Naval Reservists reported to the Custom House through the morning and gathered on the Quay in the afternoon and made their way to Southtown Station headed by a red ensign carried on a boat hook. Many were accompanied by their wives and in some instances the departing men carried their youngsters shoulder high as they were cheered along the way by crowds mostly made up of holiday visitors. As they passed the river steam boats moored at the Town Hall quay they were given a farewell salvo from their steam whistles.

On the world's stage on Monday 3 August the situation was that Germany had requested that Belgium let its troops pass through but Belgium had categorically refused and asked Britain to intervene and request an assurance that Belgian wishes would be respected. The request had been sent and the world watched and waited for the response. In England it was the August Bank Holiday and the seaside resorts of Norfolk were densely thronged with visitors, to the degree that as early as 8 August *The Yarmouth Mercury* commented 'it was difficult to realise that we were on the verge of war'. Some events, such as the Holkham Cricket week were cancelled 'in the light of the international situation.' Herbert Leeds captures the atmosphere of the day in the county before war broke out: 'beneath the surface jollity of the day there brooded a spirit of disquietude, which deepened as the hours passed and no reply was received from Germany to the English request... Throughout the day people continuously gathered in front of the offices of the *Eastern Daily Press* at Norwich, Yarmouth, Cromer and Lowestoft, where the latest bulletins were posted. Fluctuations of hope noticeable during the day began to settle at nightfall into a fixed feeling that the worst must be expected. In the hot night groups stood about the streets discussing the likely developments of the morrow.' Despite official warnings against hoarding provision merchants had a massive increase in sales of tinned food and comments were made in the press about how the prices were creeping up and unnecessary shortages being caused. Some towns were better prepared than others; foremost was Sheringham UDC who took direct action calling together all the provision dealers to ascertain what stocks they had on hand, what arrangement they had in place to replenish and obtained a promise from the traders that prices would not be raised more than absolutely necessary. At the same meeting a general Emergency Committee was formed 'to deal with any matters that might crop up unexpectedly.' At Yarmouth a stir was caused between eleven and midnight when the lights of the town were extinguished. Many saw this as a sign that war had come but it was later revealed a small unit of the Royal Navy had been lying off shore and needed to communicate with the authorities on land by means of a signal lamp.

On 4 August Sir Edward Grey, the Secretary of Foreign Affairs wired to the British ambassador in Berlin asking for a reply from Germany before midnight. During the day more soldiers were placed on guard at main post offices in larger towns. Throughout the evening of 4 August the crowds had gradually swollen in front of the telegraph and newspaper offices as the ultimatum deadline approached, along the coast as the light faded many lingered on the sea fronts 'where the lights of warcraft were discernible.' In the early evening almost 300 men from The Norwich Division of The National Reserve (Army) paraded at the Agricultural Hall and from them were selected those who had served in mounted units for the mobilization section. They divided by class of Reservist; those from the first class were sent direct to their old regiments, second class went to Territorial units and third class sent for Home Defence. At 11.00pm the message came that war had been declared against Germany and the streets rang with patriotic songs, the drink flowed, streamers were thrown and flags were waved. Wynne Willson, housemaster of the junior boys at Gresham's School recorded how the people of Holt received the news in his memoirs: 'About midnight I went out into the town to Rounce and Wortleys Stationery shop, where news was to be posted. It came from Cromer by a motor-cyclist, one of our day boys. It was read out – the fateful message that England had declared war against Germany at 11pm. There was a crowd in the street and an outburst of cheering, and I remember our school doctor shouting: 'Don't cheer, you don't know what you are in for!' All that night there was noise and excitement: boy scouts were cycling about calling up reservists and territorials...' Another man who sprang into action was Lieutenant Wenn of F Company, 5th Battalion, The Norfolk Regiment who sped around the Cromer district on his motor cycle calling up the men to report at the Armoury from 9 o'clock onwards. Those who had waited in the towns from outlying villages took it upon themselves and as a matter of pride conveyed the news to their homes and surrounding houses, hand bells were found and rung down the streets and the news relayed bellman style. When he heard the news Ben Self of Worstead, a veteran of the Chin Hills campaign and The Boer War donned his old parade helmet and pulled his scarlet tunic around his middle (only a couple of buttons would now do up) and went round the village with a makeshift drum. A number of the locals met up in the market place and by lamp light and armed with tankards of beer resolved what they would do if the Kaiser came.

The first reaction to the war situation at sea came early in the morning of 5 August when the German schooner *Fiducia* from Hamburg was seized at Yarmouth. She had been discharging her cargo of oil cake on the west side of the river at J H Bunn, no doubt as hundreds of German boats like her had done in peacetime but now we were at war and to the complete bemusement of her master Captain Mohr and her crew the boat was formally boarded by a naval officer and Custom House official and taken through the bridge to berth at Stonecutter's Quay and became the 'centre of great interest on the part of thousands of visitors and townspeople.'

Left: *Men of the Norfolk Regiment ready to entrain 1914.*

Right: *'Still open for Recruiting' The 1st East Anglian Brigade, Royal Field Artillery in front of their barracks on All Saint's Green 1914.*

On the morning of 5 August 1914 the men of the Territorial Force were mobilized and ordered to proceed to their headquarters immediately. In North Norfolk three United Automobile Services motor coaches were pressed into service leaving at a late hour on Tuesday night to collect the men of the 5th Battalion's North Norfolk company to Cromer for the early hours of Wednesday morning. Those arriving at particularly early hours were given the chance to get what sleep they could on mattresses and straw provided by A H Fox Ltd at the Parish Hall. As the men formed up in the market places to leave to leave their towns civic dignitaries and local clerics often gave a short address before the townsfolk waved off 'their brave boys' from their local detachments. In Norwich Messrs J & J Colman had placed their works club house and sporting grounds at the disposal of the military and as they already had a the ranks of a detachment filled by their men in the East Anglian Brigade Royal Field Artillery the gunners were the unit who had the benefit of this generous and commodious accommodation to muster their troops. The road area in front of the 2nd East

Norfolk Artillerymen at The Carrow Works Club House 1914.

Anglian Field Ambulance headquarters Bethel Street was soon clogged up with RAMC Territorials who were marched to the Technical and Old Middle Schools in St George's to await movement instructions. The Norfolk Yeomanry mustered at the Drill Hall on the Cattle Market. They made a smart sight on their parade at 4pm. The men who had come from outside the city would be accommodated in the Technical Institute but those who were local and provided they reported at 8am the following morning at the Drill Hall were permitted to go home and sleep in their own beds.

More National Reserves received the call-up and appeared to form a constant stream along Riverside Road and Gurney Road on their way to Britannia Barracks to rejoin the colours. The territorial infantry boys of 4th Battalion, The Norfolk Regiment were embodied at the Chapelfield Drill Hall in Norwich. Sentries were posted there all day with fixed bayonets to ensure no-one except those connected with military matters entered the building and as the day progressed Companies from outlying areas arrived in the city by train and marched up to the Drill Hall to report, drawing large cheering crowds along the way. Upon arrival the men were placed in ranks and medical inspection was carried out and the men of the Battalion were billeted on the City of Norwich Schools on Newmarket Road.

The companies of 5th Battalion, The Norfolk Regiment mustered at their Battalion Headquarters in East Dereham. At Aylsham the local Territorials paraded in the Market Place and adjourned to the Town Hall where Captain Purdy addressed his men urging upon them the importance of making themselves fit in every way, and not to grumble if they should be called upon to endure hardships. He asked them to take as their motto 'For God and the King.' The men replied with cheers. Captain Purdy then formed the men up in the Market Place where the vicar, Canon Hoare, offered up a prayer and the men marched in high spirits to the GER Station headed by the band and a number of local men fell in behind to join up and go with their pals.

The Yarmouth men of B Company took with them some 30 recruits in civvies. At Cromer the men of F Company, under the command of Capt H N Bridgewater marched from the Parish Hall to the GER station to entrain for Dereham. The *Norfolk Chronicle* reported 'All of them were in the best of spirits, and were singing with great heartiness their company song 'Roll the Chariot Along'. It was estimated by the *Lynn News* that a crowd of some 2,000 saw the Downham boys off at the station and its vicinity, especially around the crossing gates upon which boys climbed to wave off older brothers and many a local lass mopped a tear as she waved her sweetheart good-bye.

At King's Lynn despite the pelting rain the men of the Lynn Companies of 5th and 6th Battalions were given a rousing send off. The men of the 5th Battalion fell in at the Armoury on London Road and marched in batches to St James's Hall. Here they were fully equipped and to each man was given a Soldiers Pay Book – for use on active service and ammunition was brought up from the magazine under special guard. When all the men had assembled Rev. A. H. Hayes, Rector of All Saints addressed them after they had been drawn up to attention by Capt. Arthur Pattrick. After the special address and prayers the dismiss was given and he shook hands with members of the company one by one, wishing all God-speed. At the station the crowds thronged the departing

Left: *The 1st East Anglian Brigade, Royal Field Artillery muster on the Carrow Works playing fields 1914.*

Right: *Men of 2nd East Anglian Field Ambulance off to war!.*

soldiers. The Lynn boys met up with the Downham and district platoons and Hunstanton men of the 5th Battalion leaving together on the 12.30 train for East Dereham. As the train moved out to the accompaniment of cheering crowds and waving hands a young man of the 5th waved a union flag out from the window and the train blew its whistle several times, even when it had passed out of sight.

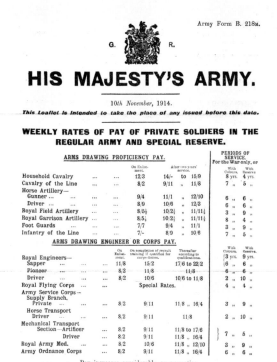

Throughout the morning of 5 August the companies of the 5th Battalion poured in to Battalion Headquarters at Dereham from Cromer, Yarmouth, Lynn, Swaffham, Downham, Sandringham and Fakenham. Because of the sheer numbers involved as the men arrived they were sent to muster in the Market Place. As the men mustered a union flag was hoisted over two businesses in the Market Place and the troops broke into loud cheers and sang 'Rule Britannia.' Each man in the battalion had to pass through the Assembly Rooms and were examined to ensure fitness and freedom from infestations and contagious diseases by Drs Belding (the Medical Officer for Health for the Dereham Urban District), Duigan and Howlett. The drill hall certainly could not accommodate all 800 men of the battalion so the maltings belonging to Messrs. F D G Smith were requisitioned for the men and the Officers accommodated on the top floor of Hobbies Ltd warehouse The place of assembly for the battalion was the Corn Hall with the Masonic Hall in Norwich Street used for stores and Assembly Rooms retained for military purposes. By nightfall of 5 August, 800 men of 5th Battalion, The Norfolk Regiment were accommodated in the town.

The 6th (Cyclist) Battalion were on their annual training camp with the 6th Suffolk Cyclists at the Pakefield Rifle Range near Lowestoft when news of standby for mobilization came from the War Office and camp was broken on 3 August. By 9pm on 4 August the cyclists were described as on a 'war footing.' On 5 August at King's Lynn the 'C' Company Cyclists formed up at their headquarters on Purfleet Quay. Rev A H Hayes prayed with them and then gave a short address then the men left for the station. As the members of the Cyclist Battalion paraded in the station yard and were just about ready for entraining the Mayor stepped forward bareheaded and addressed them. He said 'We all wish you God-speed and quick return. This is not the time for speech-making but for action and I hope you will all do your duty to your King.' Three hearty cheers for his Majesty were given on the call of the Mayor. The 6th (Cyclist) Battalion was mobilized from its headquarters and Drill Hall on the Cattle Market in Norwich. They knew that under the scheme of Home Defence prevailing in 1914 the observation and patrol of the British Coast had been entrusted to certain cycle and mounted corps of the Territorial Force. The men of the 6th had been ready and keen to proceed to their war station on 'active service' from 1100 hours but were kept waiting until after 1800 hours when the final order to proceed arrived. Very shortly after the men were ready to depart. The *Eastern Daily Press* reported 'Each man had a formidable equipment to carry that made the civilians gasp as the Territorials vaulted into the saddles

of their cycles. There were the haversack, water bottle, heavy valise, great coat, waterproof cape, a supply of ammunition (100 rounds) and rifle, the whole weighing from 20 to 30 lbs. The men, as they were making the final preparations for leaving were in the highest spirits. They sang favourite melodies with vigour and shook hands cordially with friends who came have a last word with them. And with a last whiff of their cigarettes and pipes which afforded them so much solace, and with a few smart exercises in drill, and with a fine burst of cheering they stepped gaily out the Drill Hall … girls rushed forward with merry laughter just to tap their military friends on the back, and to receive a warm glance of recognition as a reward. Umbrellas were waved in the air, handkerchiefs were flourished and all was done to make the Territorials feel that they were carrying away with them the best wishes of the people of the ancient city.' As the Cyclists rode off, smartly spaced to regulation distance they really did cut a dash, Tradesmen came quickly to their shop doors to see and people stopped, cheered and waved as the Cyclists turned the bend into Crown Road, passed across Prince of Wales Road past the bustling Territorial Association Headquarters on Tombland and onto Magdalen Street and out of the city to their 'war station' at North Walsham where they were to make their headquarters and set about patrolling the coast.

The mobilized troops in the city on the march by the Royal Hotel, Agricultural Hall Plain 1914.

    With thousands of troops mobilized they would be needing mounts, work horses and wagons. From the first mobilization order District superintendents were busy purchasing horses and baggage wagons for the use of cavalry, yeomanry and artillery. Immediately after purchase (or later, after requisition) every military horse was branded with the government mark. Many motor vehicles were also commandeered and because their use was far more important than their appearance there was a time before the pots of green paint were brought out, when groups of troops to be seen in brightly painted delivery trucks! Despite willing compliance from businesses across the county to give up some of their horses as the days passed it soon became apparent there were simply not enough horses for sale or voluntary requisition – for many farmers it was the height of harvest time; a story repeated across the country. On 8 August The Defence of the Realm Act was passed giving the government wide-

Top left: Newly acquired horses for military service, Norwich Cattle Market 1914.

Top right: Officers of XII Lancers photographed immediately before their departure to France from the Norwich Cavalry Barracks, August 1914.

ranging powers during the war period, such as censorship and the power to requisition such things as buildings, land, *horses, wagons and transport* required for the war effort. Harvest or not the army needed horses and soon cars carrying officers and perhaps a farrier sergeant with a keen eye were bouncing along the streets of city and town, rural roads and rutted country lanes in search of suitable horses and wagons to be requisitioned. Rule of thumb was applied that a small farm should only require one horse. Many farmers complained bitterly at this imposition but a horse would only be returned upon submission of a written deposition that clearly showed hardship had been caused by the loss of a working animal. Nationally 165,000 horses were drafted into service – very few were returned after hardship plea or war service.

Officers and men of XII Lancers trotting into the yard of Thorpe Station on 16 August 1914 ready to load their horses into railway cattle trucks and the men into carriages and set out on their journey to the Western Front.

Troops from 1/1st Nottinghamshire Yeomanry and their remounts at Weybourne November 1914.

3 Defence of the Realm

'He who old England hope to win,
Must at Weybourne Hope begin'
Old Norfolk couplet

When war was declared in 1914 Germany, and indeed the German people had been well established in many British minds as an aggressive, brash, haughty and militaristic people who could not be trusted. Since the late 19th century Germany had fallen from grace on the international stage and was regularly panned by the British press. The expansion of her Navy was seen as a direct challenge to the Naval might of Great Britain and a threat to our Empire. Germany had made a heavy handed and unwanted intervention during the Boxer Rebellion of 1900 and employed 'gunboat diplomacy' during the Agadir crisis of 1911 when they sent their warship *Panther* to the Moroccan port of Agadir as a display of force and a protest against French influence in Morocco and the Congo.

Troops marching along Cromer sea front 1914.

Anglo–German tensions were especially high at this time since the Germans had started to attempt to surpass Britain's naval supremacy. When the British heard of the *Panther*'s arrival in Morocco, an assumption was made that the Germans meant to turn Agadir into a naval base on the Atlantic. In the light of this event David Lloyd George, then British Chancellor of the Exchequer used

On 10 August 1914 over a thousand troops from The Essex Regiment crammed into Norwich Market Place. They even brought some alleged German spies with them (German waiters) 'captured' at Cromer.

Left: *Never to miss an opportunity Norwich barbers could see many of these troops could do with a military hair cut and brought their chairs out.*

Right: *The men of the Essex Regiment drew a great crowd and the ice cream 'Johnnies' made a fortune from the onlookers.*

the occasion of his speech at Mansion House to deliver a stern warning against further German expansion. The main result was to increase British fear and hostility and to draw Britain closer to France and reinforced the Entente Cordiale of 1904.

Furthermore, the distrust and perception of anti-British and sinister machinations of the of the German race were soon featured in popular literature. In *Riddle of the Sands*(1903) Erskine Childers weaves a tale of two young amateur sailors who battle the secret forces of mighty Germany. Their navigational skills prove as important as their powers of deduction in uncovering the sinister plot that looms over the international community. Other titles such as *The Invasion of 1910* (1906) and *Spies of the Kaiser* (1909) both by William le Queux ably demonstrate the tenor of such literature which reached its zenith in the early years of the war with John Buchan's *Thirty-Nine Steps* (1915).

Ready for duties, a section of the Essex Regiment in front of the cattle market, Norwich 1914.

Within hours of war being declared anti-German outbursts saw some families purge their homes of German products: clocks, printed pictures, toys, especially trains and teddies were destroyed. Some German businesses, or rather if the name above the shop appeared to be German, or selling a large number of overtly German products instances of damage and graffiti were recorded; even the King of Prussia pub on Ipswich Road had its sign defaced and windows smashed – when repairs had been affected it re-opened as the King George V, indeed the King himself was somewhat concerned about the clear German lineage of his surname and changed it to Windsor! And let us not forget our

beloved county was surrounded by what was they known as the German Ocean – that too was changed initially to the British Ocean, known better today as the North Sea.

On 8 August 1914 the Defence of the Realm Act (DORA) was passed; as we have seen its powers were wide ranging but above all the media and public imagination was caught by the clauses of the act which covered national security and the role they as good citizens could play in this crucial time of war:

Top left: The soldiers of The Essex Regiment marching down Duke Street 1914.

Top right: Billets at last! At Low Farm, St Faiths 1914.

In the stores of 4th Battalion, The Essex Regiment, Wymondham, Christmas 1914.

(a) to prevent persons communicating with the enemy or obtaining information for that purpose or any purpose calculated to jeopardise the success of the operations of any of His Majesty's forces or the forces of his allies or to assist the enemy; or

(b) to secure the safety of His Majesty's forces and ships and the safety of any means of communication and of railways, ports, and harbours; or

(c) to prevent the spread of false reports or reports likely to cause disaffection to His Majesty or to interfere with the success of His Majesty's forces by land or sea or to prejudice His Majesty's relations with foreign powers; or

(d) to secure the navigation of vessels in accordance with directions given by or under the authority of the Admiralty; or

(e) otherwise to prevent assistance being given to the enemy or the successful prosecution of the war being endangered.

3 Section, A Company, 6th (Cyclist) Battalion, The Norfolk Regiment, Horsey, Christmas 1914.

The Defence of the Realm Act alien registration schedule for Norfolk.

Defence of the Realm (Consolidation) Regulations, 1914.

PART OF THE

COUNTY OF NORFOLK.

Order as to Registration of
NEW RESIDENTS AND VISITORS.

WHEREAS an Order under Regulation 53 of the Defence of the Realm (Consolidation) Regulations, 1914, has been made by General Sir H. L. SMITH-DORRIEN, G.C.B., G.C.M.G., D.S.O., a Competent Military Authority under the said Regulations.

NOTICE IS HEREBY GIVEN that:—

1. (a) Every person in the area specified in the first Schedule hereto who at the date hereof is not a permanent resident therein, and (b) every person who at any time after midnight on the 6th day of August, 1915, shall arrive in the said area, whether to reside permanently or stay temporarily therein, shall, as to (A) forthwith, and as to (B) within twelve hours after his or her arrival in the said area, fill up one of the prescribed forms in accordance with the directions stated thereon, and transmit the same to the nearest Police Station.

2. The owner, occupier, or manager (as the case may be) of any premises at or on which any such person as aforesaid shall be residing or staying shall take all necessary steps to ascertain that every person residing or staying at or on his or her premises to whom this Order applies has complied with this Order, and shall forthwith give information at the nearest Police Station if he or she shall have reason to believe that this Order has not been complied with.

3. Any person who has filled up and transmitted one of the prescribed forms in accordance with this Order may apply at the Police Station to which such prescribed form was transmitted for a permit, which, if granted, shall exempt such person from further compliance with this Order for such period as is stated in such permit.

Any person claiming to act under any such permit as aforesaid shall, if at any time required to do so by the Competent Military Authority or any person authorized by him, or by any soldier engaged on sentry patrol or other similar duty, or by any officer of Customs and Excise, officer of police, or aliens officer, produce the permit for inspection, and if he refuses or neglects to do so he shall be guilty of an offence against the said Regulations. Any such permit as aforesaid may at any time be revoked.

4. The prescribed form hereinbefore referred to shall be that set forth in the Second Schedule hereto, and may be obtained at any Post Office or Police Station within the said area.

5. This Order shall remain in force during the period of the War unless previously altered or revoked.

The First Schedule.—AREA.

The areas comprised in the following Boroughs and Parishes (including detached Parishes), all situate in the County of Norfolk, namely:—The Boroughs of GREAT YARMOUTH and KING'S LYNN. The undermentioned Parishes and detached Parishes, viz.:—Walpole St. Andrew, Walpole St. Peter, Terrington St. Clement, Tilney All Saints, Tilney-cum-Islington, Tilney St. Lawrence, Clenchwarton, West Lynn, North Lynn, Mintlyn, Gaywood, Bawsey, South Wootton, North Wootton, Castle Rising, North Runcton, Roydon, West Winch, Grimston, Congham, Hillington, Babingley, Wiggenhall St. Mary, West Newton, Flitcham-cum-Appleton, Sandringham, Wolferton, Dersingham, Anmer, Shernborne, Ingoldisthorpe, Snettisham, Fring, Sedgeford, Heacham, Docking, New Hunstanton, Old Hunstanton, Ringstead, Holme-next-the-Sea, Thornham, Choseley, Titchwell, Brancaster, Burnham Deepdale, Burnham Market, Burnham Westgate, Burnham Norton, Burnham Overy, Burnham Thorpe, Burnham Sutton, North Creake, Holkham, Wells-next-the-Sea, Wighton, Little Walsingham, Great Walsingham, Waterden, Egmere, Stanhoe, Quarles, Warham St. Mary, Warham All Saints, Stiffkey, Binham, Cockthorpe, Hindringham, Morston, Langham, Blakeney, Field Dalling, Bale, Saxlingham, Wiveton, Cley-next-the-Sea, Glandford-with-Bayfield, Letheringsett, Thornage, Sharrington, Salthouse, Kelling, Holt, Weybourne, Upper Sheringham, Sheringham, Bodham, Hempstead, Edgefield, East Beckham, West Beckham. North Barningham, Town Barningham, Plumstead, Matlaske, Aldborough, Thurgarton, Baconsthorpe, Sustead, Aylmerton, Beeston Regis, Runton, Bessingham, Gresham, Cromer, Overstrand, Northrepps, Felbrigg, Metton, Roughton, Hanworth, Alby-with-Thwaite, Gunton, Thorpe Market, Southrepps, Sidestrand, Trimingham, Gimingham, Trunch, Antingham, North Walsham, Felmingham, Knapton, Bradfield, Swafield, Mundesley, Paston, Bacton, Edingthorpe, Witton, Honing, Smallburgh, Dilham, East Ruston, Walcot, Happisburgh, Stalham, Worstead, Ridlington, Crostwight, Brunstead, Lessingham, Hempstead-with-Eccles, Ingham, Palling, Barton Turf, Sutton, Waxham, Hickling, Catfield, Potter Heigham, Horsey, Repps-cum-Bastwick, Martham, West Somerton, East Somerton, Winterton, Hemsby, Rollesby, Ashby-with-Oby, Ormesby St. Michael, Ormesby St. Margaret with Scratby, Burgh St. Margaret, Filby, Caister-next-Yarmouth, Thrigby, Stokesby-with-Herringby, Mautby, Runham, Halvergate, Wickhampton, Reedham, Haddiscoe, Whealacre, Aldeby, Burgh St. Peter, Thorpe St. Andrew, Postwick, Whitlingham, Brundall, Surlingham, Strumpshaw, Buckenham, Claxton, Carleton St. Peter, Langley, Cantley, Hardley, Norton Subcourse, Thurlton, Thorpe-next-Haddiscoe, Gillingham, Geldeston, Ellingham, Broome, Ditchingham, Limpenhoe, Freethorpe, Moulton, Tunstall, Beighton, Acle, Blofield, Hemblington, South Walsham, Upton-with-Fishley, Ranworth-with-Panxworth, Billockby, Clippesby, Thurne, Ludham, Horning, Irstead, Tunstead, Hoveton St. Peter, Seo Ruston, Coltishall, Horstead-with-Stanninghall, Belaugh, Wroxham, Salhouse, Hoveton St. John, Woodbastwick, Neatishead, Beeston St. Lawrence, Kirby Bedon, Bramerton. DETACHED PARISHES:—Cantley, Acle (Nos. 1, 2, and 3), Postwick, Burlingham St. Andrew, Runham, Runham Vauxhall, South Walsham, Beighton, Freethorpe, Moulton, Langley, Chedgrave (No. 2), Stockton (Nos. 1, 2, 3, 4, and 5), Toft Monks (Nos. 1 and 2).

The Second Schedule.—NORFOLK SPECIAL AREA.

1. Present address in the area.
2. Date of arrival in the area.
3. Surname.
4. Christian name.
5. Nationality.
6. Sex (male or female).
7. Permanent address (a) Residence, (b) Business.
8. Rank or occupation.
9. Birthplace.
10. Year of birth.
11. Whether served in any Army, Navy, or Police Force. If so, state what Army, Navy, or Police Force.
12. Arrived here from (give last address in full).
13. Date of intended departure from the area.
14. Intended new address on departure from the area.

Signature of person to whom the above particulars relate.............................

Combine this with The Aliens Registration Act (1914) that made the registration of all aliens over the age of 16 with the police mandatory and you have a green light for every patriotic Britain to root out 'enemy aliens,' German sympathisers and spies. Under these draconian charters the police and military authorities had their work cut out for them. In the opening months of the war nationally 6,000 properties were searched, 120,000 reported cases of 'suspicious activity' investigated and many migrants and those who had fled the war from the continent, some 9,000 of them all told, were interned and held in special detention camps.

But then, spies could be anywhere. In July 1908, *The Times* reported how the Secretary of State for War was asked in Parliament whether he could say anything concerning 'a staff ride through England organised by a foreign power' and whether he had 'received any official information or reports from chief constables in the Eastern Counties as to espionage in England by foreign nations.' In 1909 Haldane had set up and personally chaired a subcommittee of the Committee of Imperial Defence to consider 'the nature and extent of the foreign espionage that is at present taking place in the country.' In a report presented to this committee by Colonel James Edmonds head of MO5, which ran the 'Special Section' of the War Office, twelve cases of 'alleged reconnaissance work by Germans' – among them the report from a Norfolk inn-keeper who had 'two foreigners, stoutish, well-set-up men' who had called at his establishment. Another informant reported 'individuals, unmistakably foreigners' who were 'too absorbed and businesslike for ordinary tourists' in the North Walsham area.

In April 1909 there was much talk about powered flight and there was great excitement about the forthcoming cross channel flight attempt by Louis Bleriot in his monoplane – but that was set for a few

months away in July perhaps this set more minds wondering about the Germans and *their* new aircraft – the mighty and ominous looking Zeppelin? The first reports of an airship flying over Norfolk in the hours of darkness was made on 21 April 1909 when a witness who saw it flying over New Common Marsh Farm and going across the Wash towards Hunstanton gave his account of the sighting to the *Daily Express*. On 16 May 'lights of an airship' were reported over the Norfolk Broads. At dusk on May 19 an 'airship' was spotted manoeuvring at a great altitude over Shoeburyness in Essex by a Royal Artillery Sergeant. At 11.30pm the same night a 'well-known resident' was riding a motorbike over Wroxham Bridge when the lamp on his machine suddenly went out. Dismounting to examine the lamp, the rider was suddenly hit by a "dazzling" flashlight beam which appeared to be directed upon him from the sky above. Shortly after this, Mrs Turner of New Catton saw 'a flash of light which made the street look like day.' In her account she described a noise like 'the whirring of wheels' and enlarges; 'I looked up and there I saw a big star of light in front and a big searchlight behind... It was coming from the NNE from the direction of the Angel Road School and flying very low, so low that it would have touched the pinnacle of the school had it passed directly over it.' Nearer midnight, a torpedo-shaped airship with a powerful searchlight was distinctly observed by a man riding a bicycle at Tharston, south of Norwich. Shortly afterwards a group of people in Framlingham, Suffolk, claimed they saw a similar aerial object. What did these people see independently and so many miles apart?

Questions were asked in the House of Commons and Mr Fell, the MP for Great Yarmouth asked the Secretary of State for War if he could give the numbers of dirigibles constructed or in the course of construction by Germany. Haldane replied that seven dirigible airships had been built, and another five were under construction. A further question from a Mr Myer to Haldane enquired: 'Will the honourable gentleman, in any report he may circulate, tell us about a certain dirigible supposed to be hovering about our coast?' This question was greeted with laughter, and no reply was given.

On the outbreak of war in 1914 numerous instances of suspicious characters and potential spies were reported to the authorities. A typical case was reported in the *Dereham and Fakenham Times* of Saturday 22 August 1914: 'On Tuesday morning a very smart caravan of the type used by holidaymakers drawn by two stout horses had been noticed on the coast and very early in the morning was observed at Weybourne at the time an aeroplane alighted to leave a message... approaching noon a young violinist made his appearance in Blakeney and the excellent music he played induced a musician who is a summer resident to solicit permission to examine the violin. The examination revealed some uncommon features and the violinists answers to searching questions addressed to him being unsatisfactory the gentleman felt it his duty to convey certain suspicions he had formed to the authorities, who were soon on the track of the musician and likewise the caravan, which was found in the neighbourhood of Morston. Inside were found two men and a woman. A search revealed sufficient to cause the detention of the entire party. The musician and a second man were detained at Morston and escort of our Territorials conveyed the caravan and the remainder of the party to Holt... on the heels of this came the news that on the same day a motor car containing three persons, which had been carefully noted had been bagged between Sheringham and Weybourne.'

Norwich City Police Special Constables on parade on Chapel Field Gardens in August 1917.

With pressure put on the police to deal with potential enemy aliens, spies and suspicious characters, chase up registrations and a host of other tasks war generates coupled with the fact that many policemen were ex-soldiers and had been called or returned to the colours the ranks of those who maintained law and order in Norfolk were in desperate need of increase. Mr J A Porter the Lord Mayor of Norwich summoned a meeting at St Andrew's Hall on 4 September 1914, a poignant date chosen deliberately because it was exactly one month after the declaration of war, with a view to alleviate the situation. The evening was met with 'enthusiastic fervour' which culminated in 419 of the men of Norwich joining the Special Constabulary. They were sworn in batches before local magistrates, and many more followed later who were sworn before the City Magistrates at the Guildhall by the end of 1914 680 specials had been 'sworn in' and at its height 714 war emergency 'specials' were on the beat in the city. The only down side for these men was they, initially, didn't look much like constables – yes they had truncheons, handcuffs had to be shared by specials going on and off duty and their 'uniform' was only an arm band on their civvy clothes. A lapel badge arrived soon after but caps did not arrive until in January 1916 and it was only in the following August they eventually got their 'full pride of blue uniform.'

Organised under the Chief Constable with the great organisational efforts of Deputy Chief Constable Hodges a total of four companies of 'specials' were formed with four commanders, eight sub-commanders and from sixty to seventy sergeants. The company command structure was:

No. 1 Company.
Commander: Mr Richard Windsor Bishop
Sub-Commanders: Edward Coe and Mr J H Ash

No. 2 Company.
Commander: Mr Ernest Edward Hines
Sub-Commanders: Mr W E Keefe and Mr E J Theobald

No. 3 Company.
Commander: Mr A T Chittock
Sub-Commanders: Rev H D Liddell and Mr A W Ward

No. 4 Company.
Commander: Mr F R C Eaton
Sub-Commanders: Mr E J Caley and Mr J Howard Dakin

The 'specials' were placed on duty at numerous 'points' with the regular constables and, in addition, were given duties of guarding vulnerable spots such as bridges and the gas and electricity works and later assisted to maintain the blackouts when air raids threatened. By way of keeping the men fit for their job and 'in step' with drill route marches were arranged from January 1917, generally on Sundays, when the men would, on their longest stretch, march from Norwich to Wroxham and Coltishall, then back to the city.

It did not take long for the people of the county of Norfolk to realise the true horrors of the new war, Norfolk men were present and fell in the opening battles in France, mourning was already known in a number of Norfolk households by the time the first train load of returned wounded arrived at Thorpe Station on 17 October 1914. In the past wars had been fought on foreign fields but modern technology brought the war to literally our doorsteps. At about 7 o'clock on the misty Tuesday morning of 3 November 1914 Great Yarmouth

Welcoming back the King's Lynn Royal Navy Reservist survivors of the sinking of Aboukir, Hogue *and* Cressy *1914.*

A historic group for the camera, King's Lynn civic dignitaries with the local Royal Navy Reservist survivors of the sinking of Aboukir, Hogue *and* Cressy *1914.*

was shelled from the sea by battleships. The ships involved in this first Imperial German Navy raid on the English coast during the Great War came from the 1st and 2nd Scouting Group viz:

1st Scouting Group
Seydlitz, Kapitan zur See von Egidy. Flag of Konteradmiral Franz Hipper.
Moltke, KzS von Levetzow
Von der Tann, KzS Hahn, Flag of KA Tapken
Blucher, Freggattenkapitan Erdmann

2nd Scouting Group
Stralsund, KzS Harder (SO of 2nd SG)
Strassburg, Fk Retzman
Graudenz, Fk Pullen
Kolberg, KzS Widenmann

Their mission was to bombard Yarmouth and lay mines off the port. The old Torpedo Gun Boat *Halcyon* was minesweeping off Yarmouth when the German forces approached and fired on her, *Halcyon* was only slightly damaged but suffered 3 wounded as a result. It could have been worse, the German gunnery

Reginald Overton, originally from Bedford Street in Norwich was killed serving as a Boy 1st Class aboard HMS Bulwark *when she accidentally blew up on 26 November 1914. All officers were killed and out of her complement of 750, only 14 sailors survived.*

Two British 'H' class submarine lie alongside their war trophy, a captured German coastal type submarine at Hall Quay, Great Yarmouth 1919.

was not good, due to poor fire distribution and excitement at their first target. A smoke screen by the escorting destroyers *Lively* and *Leopard* was also very effective.

Stralsund laid 100 mines off Smiths Knoll. HM Submarines *D3*, *D5* and *E10* had been sent out of Yarmouth with the orders to intercept the enemy off Terschelling. While proceeding on the surface to the interception point, *D5* struck a drifting mine and was sunk leaving just 5 survivors from the crew of 24; they were picked up outside the sand to the south of Gorleston by the Berwick boat *Faithful*, transferred to a waiting motor launch and sped up the river to the Crossley Hospital. The misty weather conditions meant the German's bombardment of Yarmouth was ineffective, the shells fell short of any target, the majority of their shrapnel landing on the beaches at Gorleston – all of which proved extremely tempting souvenirs for the locals. In the 1980s there were still a number of these pieces known to exist in Yarmouth and Gorleston – the author was lucky enough to be given one of them by the man who picked it up!

What diabolical action would the Germans do next? The streets filled with rumour and gossip and sightings of spies reinvigorated.

King's Lynn MP, Holcombe Ingleby, in his book *The Zeppelin Raid in West Norfolk* (1915) recounted the story told to him by Mr H C Barber, Headmaster of Glebe House Preparatory School (and further mentioned by a Mr Blatchford in the *Weekly Despatch*) of two suspicious characters dressed as soldiers who stayed at the Sandringham Hotel in Hunstanton around 7 November 1914: 'The soldiers attracted attention in the dining room that night by their unmannerly behaviour. They came in late and stood for a long time with their caps on. The other guests were indignant; but curiosity seems to have overridden indignation, and later they fell into conversation with the strangers, and particularly with the sergeant.' Their behaviour of the two men became even more bizarre – they borrowed a car from a fellow resident, under the condition they took the chauffeur with them but the owner could not come because it was 'against regulations.' Starting off towards Brancaster they passed a young constable on duty at Old Hunstanton, commandeered him and took him along. Arriving at Titchwell they turned off down the short strip of road which led to the church and rectory. Leaving constable and chauffeur to guard the machine the soldiers made off past the rectory. The vicars' daughter spotted the men and raised the alarm. Challenged by the vicar the response was 'a flood of Billingsgate.' The vicar then informed the men he was also a Special Constable the sergeant then, with stick in hand, closed on the vicar and accused him of being a spy and threatened to arrest him. The rector held his ground and the sergeant assumed a more conciliatory attitude, keeping up his military attitude he asked the rector if he had seen any flashing thereabouts. Bluffing his way out of the situation the sergeant returned to the car and they began their odyssey again travelling to Wells and back again. The constable was to comment the sergeant certainly knew the roads of the coast better than he did. The following morning the police inspector, none too pleased at having one of his officers commandeered in such a manner went to see the men in the hotel, but strangely the men were not detained.' Ingleby points out, 'It is only fair to add that, according to the statement received by me, the inspector would have detained the suspects but for instructions from headquarters. On the night of their departure there was a big scare on the East Coast, and troops were under arms all night. It may be presumed that the visit to Hunstanton of these 'gentlemen' in khaki had some serious and definite purpose.'

At this same time a Mrs Hooks of Heacham came across a car stationed on the road above Heacham Bottom. Its purpose, she said, was signalling and she saw 'two long upward flashes and one short one, followed by two horizontal flashes. Her concerns were reported to the local constable. It was not to be the first or the last reported case of flash signalling and other witnesses named Geoffrey Girling and William Playford were willing to attest to they saw from the Heacham and Snettisham Hill area.

Although the damage caused by the shelling of Great Yarmouth had been minimal, the immediacy and warning of what could happen next time could not and would not be ignored and far more destructive bombardments of Hartlepool and Scarborough in December 1914 did nothing to quiet the fears of Norfolk people. Despite the press hyping the actions at Mons, it was clear the war was not going to be easily won and really could not be 'all over by Christmas' as had been vaunted in those halcyon days of early August 1914 and there was much talk of invasion. On the outbreak of hostilities the civil authorities had no directives as to their course of action in the event of invasion but Local Emergency Committees were set up in each parish across the county under the direction of the Lord Lieutenant. The chief duty of the Emergency Committees was that of planning with the local military authorities the necessary measures to be adopted in the locality for the facilitating the operations of HM forces and the hindrance of the enemy and provision of the organisation necessary to carry out those measures – such as digging trenches, the construction of road blocks, and obtaining lists of motorised vehicles that could be used to assist in the event of an evacuations or in response to the needs of the military. The manpower provided for this scheme, as well as other related measures such as the provision of tools and labour for the military or for example, the removal or destruction of horses and harness or rendering vehicles unserviceable in the event of imminent invasion was drawn from and allotted to trustworthy local volunteers or special constables. In Norwich a Civilian Emergency Corps was formed for the same purpose, originally consisting of 1,600 volunteers each one of them had an allocated duty and a unique numbered white metal lapel badge surmounted by the heraldic arms of the City. The committees also ensured they had a clear invasion warning system.

With regard to the civil population, it was recognised that although the military authorities considered it preferable that people stayed where they were except in case of heavy bombardment, this really would not be practical – a planned and organised evacuation was infinitely more preferable to a mass exodus in panic so posters and handbills were prepared showing the roads which would be closed

Badge of the Norwich Civilian Emergency Corps.

Evacuation routes from Great Yarmouth in the event of bombardment or invasion, issued to householders in February 1915.

KEEP THIS IN A PROMINENT PLACE.

Directions to the Public in the event of Bombardment or Invasion.

In case of BOMBARDMENT do NOT go into the STREET, but **keep** in your cellar or **on the ground floor of your home.**

In case of a hostile landing and the necessity arising of leaving the town, VEHICLES from **YARMOUTH** must travel by CAISTER ROAD.

FOOT PASSENGERS from Yarmouth must proceed past VAUXHALL STATION on to the ACLE NEW ROAD.

Both Vehicles and Foot Passengers from **SOUTHTOWN AND GORLESTON** must use the road to ST. OLAVES via BRADWELL AND ASHBY.

It must be borne in mind that in case of any of the roads being required for the movement of Troops, civilians must be prepared to move off the roads temporarily into adjacent fields if necessary in order that they may not hinder the movement of the Troops.

Persons leaving the Town should provide themselves with **food** and **warm clothing.**

If you wish for **advice** ask one of the SPECIAL CONSTABLES who will be on duty in case of danger, and be prepared to obey the directions given to you.

If any alarm comes during school hours, the **children attending the elementary schools** will be sent home at once.

DAVID McCOWAN,
Mayor.

Town Hall,
Great Yarmouth.
6th February, 1915.

or open to the public. Special constables were charged with picketing the roads and maintaining order. In the 'front line' town of Great Yarmouth the 'Directions to the Public in the event of Bombardment or Invasion' were issued to householders in February 1915 with the instruction 'Keep this in a prominent place' emblazoned in bold across the top.

The General Line of evacuation of the civil population, horned stock and transport beyond 10 miles from the East Coast was approved by General Sir Horace Smith-Dorrien from 1st Army Central Force, Cambridge as follows:

No.1 Acle	To Norwich. No stock to be moved.
No.2 Aylsham	Towards King's Lynn and Terrington
No. 3 Dereham	Swaffham and Downham Market
No. 4 Docking	To King's Lynn and Terrington
No.5 Downham	To March
No. 6 Harling	To Thetford and Newmarket
No.7 Holt	Rudham, Hillington, King's Lynn and Terrington
No.8 Loddon	North of Loddon, Brooke to Norwich. South of that line to New Buckenham, Harling and Thetford
No.9 North Walsham	To Norwich
No.10 Norwich	East of Norwich to Norwich. Rest to Hingham and Watton
No.11 Pulham	To Harling, Thetford and Newmarket
No. 12 Swaffham	To Downham Market and March
No. 13 Terrington	If necessary, to Wisbeach or Spalding way.
No.14 Walsingham	To King's Lynn and Terrington
No. 15 Wymondham	To Hingham, Watton, Mundford and Littleford
No. 16 Norwich	To remain. But those removing to go via Hingham, Watton and Mundford
No.17 Yarmouth	If the landing is in Norfolk to go via Suffolk. If the landing is in Suffolk go via Acle to Norwich
No. 18 King's Lynn	Through Terrington to Wisbech or Spalding way.

Similar plans entitled *Emergency Arrangements & Instructions to be Carried Out in Event of Invasion* were also sent to the local railway companies in 1916, marked 'Secret.' The orders for the GER were clear:

i. All trains other than those required to be run by the military authorities proceeding towards the threatened area to be stopped and disposed of.

ii. All trains at other than those required to be run by the military authorities running in the threatened area to be worked out of that area with all despatch

iii. All engines at Stations upon the Coast or within 20 miles thereof within the threatened area must, unless otherwise decided by the military authorities be removed to depots beyond the 20 miles limit.

iv. The clearance of coast stations within the threatened area must have the first consideration, and after this has been done the station nearest the coast should be cleared gradually up to the 20 mile limit

v. Engines under repair or out of steam, which cannot be hauled away, must be rendered unworkable and incapable of rapid repair

vi. As many of the civil population as possible may be conveyed, if they present themselves for that purpose, in both passenger and goods vehicles, but trains must not be delayed or stopped for picking up passengers.

There then followed a list of GER Stations and a list of where they should be removed to, the entries for Norfolk show:

Hunstanton and Kings Lynn . . . . remove to Peterborough and beyond
Swaffham, Wells, Dereham,
Sheringham, Cromer, Mundesley,
Norwich, Yarmouth Vauxhall . . . . remove to Wymondham and beyond
Yarmouth South Town . . . . remove to Tivetshall and beyond

On the outbreak of war young men rushed to join the colours, ladies volunteered for work with the Red Cross and war charities but there remained a considerable body of men, officially too old for military service, who felt they could do something more to help their country. Across Great Britain examples of local groups of men, normally led by a local retired ex-army officer gathered together to form units for local defence in the event of the enemy coming to their town or village. Although this was not part of the official Emergency Committee directives such groups were usually created with the knowledge of the committee, and there could well have been some who were members of both. Examples of such early units could be found in Holt, Swaffham, Attleborough and Great Yarmouth. The military authorities and government were not entirely comfortable with the idea of unregulated bands of armed men roaming the countryside, no matter how patriotic they may be, and very soon began organising an official national volunteer scheme. Other areas did not go as far as setting up unofficial units but certainly the desire to do *something* proactive

The lapel badge of the Great Yarmouth VTC 1914.

The Holt VTC on parade upon the Gresham's School sports field – armed with the school OTC rifles.

on a local basis in the interests of 'Home Defence' were suggested in parish minutes and in press correspondence. In the case of Norwich it was Mr W E Keefe who began the correspondence in the *Eastern Daily Press* and supported by Malcom Caley (of the chocolate manufacturing family) in November 1914. The corps was established at a meeting held in the Assembly Room of the Agricultural Hall on 4 December with Mr Francis Hornor, Sheriff of Norwich, presiding. A total of 276 names of volunteers were collected and an appeal for more was launched and after an agreed approach, the well respected Lt Colonel Leathes Prior VD accepted the post of the unit's first commandant, but volunteers remained democratic, the men came from all walks of life, a committee was set up and every subsequent officer began as a member of the ranks and file. As W. G. Clarke recalled in *Home Defence: The Norwich Volunteers:* 'Inspired by a sense of duty, and a desire not to be compelled to

*The first parade of the
Norwich Volunteer
Training Corps, 15
December 1914.*

remain hapless in case of an invasion of East Anglia grey-bearded veterans vied
with active men of middle age in learning the mysteries of drill. Bricklayers
jostled doctors; clergymen, solicitors, architects and men who had given long
years service to the city rubbed shoulders with penurious patriots.'

*The Norwich VTC
Cyclist Company on
parade at All Saint's
Green 1915.*

*The Thetford VTC in
1915.*

Joining regulations were clear; membership was restricted to 'able' men over 38 years of age (it was later raised by the War Office to 41) who were not eligible for service in the Regular or Territorial Forces. The first parade of the Norwich Volunteer Training Corps (VTC) mustered in the market place and marched to the Chapel Field Drill Hall on 15 December 1914, where it was announced 550 men had enrolled to date, the names of new members published day by day by favour of the *Eastern Daily Press*. By January 1915, there were twenty-eight squads drilling three times a week in various public buildings around the city and afternoon drills on Thursdays and Saturdays on the Earlham Road Recreation Ground. Clarke continues: in the effort to 'form fours,' about turn, left incline and on the right form squad with a precision that should give some encouragement to the long-suffering drill instructors. All were anxious to learn, but at sixty a man who has never had an hours' drill in his life finds a difficulty in deciding which is right and which left with sufficient rapidity to make a squad or platoon move as one man.' Their senior instructor, Colour Sergeant B. T. Bokenham certainly had his work cut out for him. Initially the men did not have uniforms except a red arm band marked 'G R' in black letters but still they took their training seriously and turned out in their civvies, regularly assembled in Norwich Market Place and proceeded on route marches. In any society there will be the sceptics or those who simply find some satisfaction in their derisory comments and soon some were referring to the volunteers as 'The Cripple's Brigade,' certainly a bit harsh when one considers the average age of the average age of a Norwich VTC volunteer was 44 but that said, the recruiting booklets were at pains to point out 'First-class Life and Accident insurance offices are quite willing that service in the Volunteers shall not invalidate their policies.'

On 30 January 1915 Malcom Caley, who had been appointed Adjutant, announced the volunteers had now enough members to form a battalion consisting of A, B, C, D, E, and Cyclist companies with specialist sections for signals, transport and ambulance. Early in 1915 a bugle band was formed under Bugler Sergeant T M Woods, fifty Martini rifles were purchased and a public appeal for funds met with a generous response. In the same year the VTCs from across the county were amalgamated to form The Norfolk Volunteers. The City of Norwich Volunteers became officially designated the 1st (City of Norwich) Battalion, Norfolk Volunteers. Soon uniforms were issued and even cap badges were struck – the county men had 'The Norfolk Volunteers' but Norwich retained, with some pride, 'City of Norwich Volunteers' as the legend in the scroll under their badge.

Left: Uniforms at last. The 1st (City of Norwich) Battalion, Norfolk Volunteers being inspected by the Earl of Leicester, accompanied by Lt Col Leathes Prior VD, 26 September 1915.

Right: A little thank-you sent to Mrs Pillow for her donation to the funds of The City of Norwich Volunteers.

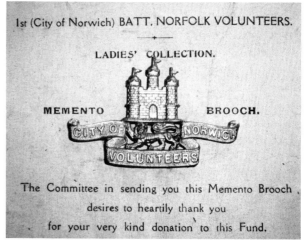

The 1st (City of Norwich) Battalion, Norfolk Volunteers (as at late 1915)

'A' Company
Company Commander: H. Harper Smith
Platoon Commanders:
  A. D. Sutton
  Dr E. I. Watson
  R. W. Collinson
  F. W. W. Morgan
Company Sergeant Major: E T Fish
Company Quarter Master Sergeant: R. Nelson
Platoon Sergeants:
  C W Thaine
  R Peck
  R J Burton (Musketry Instructor)

'B' Company
Company Commander: C. Raymond Wheeler
Platoon Commanders:
  Rev. B. Mahon
  H. Oake
Company Sergeant Major: H C Emms
Company Quarter Master Sergeant: J. Holford
Platoon Sergeants:
  A J Chettleburgh
  F W Haydon

'C' Company
Company Commander: Major J. Fildes
Platoon Commanders:
  F M Long
  J Wilkinson
  A W F Bagge
  T Lakey (Signal Section)
Company Sergeant Major: S Chesterton
Company Quarter Master Sergeant: P A Thouless

Platoon Sergeants:
  H Bradberry
  C F Butcher
  A Edwards
  W Holdsworth

'D' Company
Company Commander: Captain Vivian E. Turner
Platoon Commanders:
  H H Halls
  A H Plowright
  F J W Oakley
  W C Webster

Company Sergeant Major: C S Morley
Company Quarter Master Sergeant: G Spalding
  & Rev G N Herbert

'E' Company (in formation)
Platoon Commander: F S Culley

Cyclist Company
Company Commander: E. Bailey Page
Platoon Commanders:
  H Bryan
  F E Smith
Company Quarter Master Sergeant:
  G E W Woolsey
Platoon Sergeants:
  F W Morris
  A. St Quinton
Transport Officer: J. Gerald Snelling
Quarter Master: Capt. F Ray
Recruiting Officer: H. Newhouse

Primarily the Norfolk Volunteers were concerned with conducting patrols and providing sentries for the likes of bridges, tunnels, utility works and even important stretches of railway – from nine or ten in the evening until six in the morning they kept their vigil in case of sabotage, suspicious characters being seen or even to warn of landings and invasion.

The Transport Section of the City of Norwich Volunteers 1915.

The Mulbarton & District company of the Norfolk Volunteers 1916.

Platoon Commander W C Webster, 'D' Company, City of Norwich Volunteers 1915.

One of the Great Yarmouth Company of The Norfolk Volunteers.

The War Office and Admiralty were both keen to utilise the services of the Volunteers so detachments from across the county were employed in such duties as guarding, constructing defensive earthworks and assisting ground crew with the movement of aircraft on airfields such as Bacton or, eventually, airships at Pulham. The City of Norwich boys (and some from Norfolk Volunteer Battalions such as Attleborough) got to Pulham by a special train chartered by the Admiralty and would march to the air station headed by their band and the locals often came out to give them a wave and a cheer as they passed by. The work, however, was hard as they were initially helping to prepare the ground for the construction of the air station. They grubbed up hedges and filled ditches, initially the men even had to take their own tools! Much of the work of digging the cutting for the permanent way of the railway that connected the site with the line at Pulham Market was carried out by the Volunteers.

Once established the Norwich Volunteers had a headquarters at the historic Howard House on King Street and they took part in more advanced training on the miniature rifle range set up in Mountergate and out on manoeuvres. In December 1915 Norfolk Volunteers combined for an exercise –

Three of the Norfolk Volunteers during manoeuvres.

Parade of the Norfolk Volunteers at Norwich Cathedral 1916.

'The Battle of Caistor' in which they divided into two 'armies' one of which attempted to force the passage of the River Tas at Markshall, while the other defended it. It was recorded as 'a great fight, but the only casualty was a rabbit, which one of the attackers accidently fell on and killed while coming through a plantation.' A later exercise at Swainsthorpe saw a conveyance of stores on a wagon with the cyclist company charged with finding the road selected and preparing and ambush in the

Time for refreshment for the Norfolk Volunteers 'in the field' 1915.

most suitable spot. There ended with a great disparity of numbers and more cyclists were used in the attack than anticipated; cyclists triumphant, the victors proceeded to the crossroads near the village and amicably divided the spoils of the rations.

In the latter years of the war, efforts were made to increase the military efficiency of the volunteers: they were formally 'sworn in' and had to pass a standard of health and physique. When conscription was introduced in 1916 their numbers were bolstered further when exemption from military service was granted for those in reserved occupations – on condition they joined the volunteers. But, somewhat sadly, no matter what they did the old sobriquet of 'England's Last Hope' seemed to stick to The Norfolk Volunteers; a nick-name, with others, which was to be applied again to their next incarnation as Local Defence Volunteers in 1940.

Defences

In the Norwich Volunteers recruiting booklet of 1916, they illustrated a map showing Norwich as the centre point for a compass and drew a circle which within its radius encompassed Derby, Sheffield, Calais and Ostend. With this visual aid they clearly demonstrated the war (and German occupation) was as far away from us in Norfolk as a few northern cities and posed the question – 'Do you realise how near we are at Norwich from the scene of actual warfare? Later in the publication they explore why Norwich needs to have a defence force and explained it as: 'She (Norwich) recognises that the great war is a life and death struggle – we must win or go under. She recognises our enemies kill our wounded, ill-treat our prisoners, bombard our watering places, air raid our East Coast towns and villages, introduced poison gas and use every other contrivance inevitable only of the devil himself. Our Grant Fleet so far had shielded us from even worse calamities. The kultured bipeds from Germany have not yet been able to put a foot on our soil.' The tirade then cites peacetime statistics from Germany which illustrate their 'monstrosity.' Alongside the expected stats of murder, felonious wounding, malicious damage, arson, rape, incest and 'unnatural crimes' are shown the stats for illegitimate children and divorce petitions: all sinister and distasteful stuff to 'polite and decent' British society. With deadlock in the trenches and indecisive outcomes of naval engagements the pressure was on from the British people to build our defences against the invader, a threat very much in the minds of Norfolk people. The deep waters and natural harbours of the North Norfolk coast could make easy landing grounds for invaders.

Such fears had been known through history, the Romans and Vikings made landings here, extensive defence plans had been drawn up for the county to

The newly adopted battalion mascot of the 1/1st Nottinghamshire Yeomanry, Weybourne 1914.

combat the Spanish Armada in 1588 and again during the Napoleonic Wars – the old couplet:

> 'He who old England hope to win,
> Must at Weybourne Hope begin'

was oft repeated, and very true. Weybourne was one of the 'gateways' of invasion and thus troops had been encamped there since the first month of the war. In December 1914 Sydney Cozens-Hardy wrote from Letheringsett to his brother, Baron Herbert Cozens-Hardy, Master of the Rolls relating the supposed invasion plans of Germans related to him by the senior local officers: 'The Germans have specially constructed flat-bottom boats each of which holds 3 trains and there is accommodation in these boats for 40,000 men. The plan they (the local officers) believe is for the boat to land the men at Sheringham and hide under the cliffs until they are all landed.' However, he does add 'It is doubtful these boats can live in a rough sea.' By the end of 1914 first line trenches were dug across the Sheringham Golf Links; indeed, between Weybourne and Salthouse eleven defensive positions overlooked the beach, manned by four companies, there were thirty trenches running from Gallow Hill to Weybourne Mill and in strategic areas in the countryside between Sheringham and Holt with further trench systems dug around Sea Palling and around Yarmouth and Gorleston. Second and third line trenches to back these up were also dug near Aylsham and between Hunworth and Briston; as a further anti-invasion measure the marshes at Salthouse were allowed to flood. The coastline from Wells to Gorleston was patrolled by our gallant territorial boys of 6th (Cyclist) Battalion, The Norfolk Regiment; mobile troops for quick response in the event of invasion from the Yeomanry of the 1st and 2nd Mounted Divisions which had been deployed to the county, such as the 1/1st Glamorgan Yeomanry and 1/1st Pembroke Yeomanry at Aylsham or 1/1st County of London Yeomanry in the North Walsham area.

Heavy Batteries consisting of six 60-pounders of the Royal Field Artillery were stationed at Weybourne and Mundesley. There were also two 4.7-inch guns

A Squadron, 1/1st Montgomeryshire Yeomanry at Blickling Hall 1915.

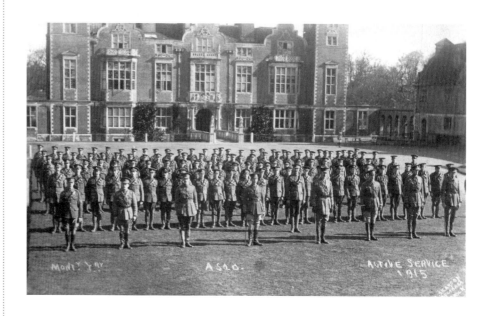

on travelling carriages stationed at Cromer and a single in an entrenchment on Gorleston cliffs. Two 15-pounders were manned at Salthouse and further same calibre guns were set up in small emplacements at Eccles, Newport and Caister. None of this artillery could have sunk a battleship but rather was intended as the heavy armour to harry an invasion force as it disembarked. There was also an armoured train (one of just two in the entire country) consisting of four armoured wagons armed with two 12-pounder guns and two machines guns, which ran along the M&GN branch line to Mundesley with occasional trips as far afield as Yarmouth and Lowestoft.

Some of the earliest fixed defences in the country were constructed in Norfolk. Begun in 1916/17 the first major generation of these fixed defences were constructed from concrete blocks with heavy steel doors and loopholes with steel shutters behind that could be raised or dropped as necessary; circular in design with a flat roof this design gave raise to their nickname of 'pillboxes' – a *nom de guerre* which has stuck to such defences ever since, no matter what their shape. Built to supplement the existing trench lines along the Norfolk coast,

Left: *Members of 1/1st Glamorgan Yeomanry in the stables at Aylsham 1915.*

Right: *Men of the 1/1st Montgomeryshire Yeomanry having a 'knock-about' boxing match, Aylsham 1915.*

Men of the East Anglian Royal Field Artillery Battery, Stalham 1915.

Bottom left: *B Squadron of the 2/1st County of London Yeomanry (Middlesex Hussars) after digging entrenchments near Aylsham, summer 1916.*

Bottom centre: *A smart machine gun crew from the Lincolnshire Yeomanry manning a Maxim 08 on the rifle range at Garboldisham 1915.*

Bottom right: *Troops from the Lincolnshire Yeomanry at the Garboldisham rifle range 1915.*

Top left: *Artillerymen manoeuvre a gun carriage through the streets of East Dereham c1914.*

Bottom left: *The Battalion support vehicle of 2/6th (Cyclist) Battalion, The Royal Sussex Regiment at Winterton 1915.*

Top right: *Camp of the 2/6th (Cyclist) Battalion, The Royal Sussex Regiment in the field opposite Mill House on the old Yarmouth Road, Stalham, August 1915.*

Bottom right: *2/6th (Cyclist) Battalion, Royal Sussex Regiment on the march through Stalham, August 1915.*

pillboxes were erected by companies of Royal Engineers at selected points on the coast and a short distance inland in an extended line from Stiffkey and Weybourne to Sea Palling and at almost every river crossing along the line of the river Ant from Bradfield to Wayford Bridge. Many of the river crossing defence pillboxes were constructed with their loopholes placed at different levels and

'Come to the cook house door' the men of the 1/1st East Riding of Yorkshire Yeomanry at Costessey Hall park. This unit was part of the North Midland Mounted Brigade, 1st Mounted Divsion based in Norfolk from May to October 1915.

Top left: *The Farriers of 2/1st Derbyshire Imperial Yeomanry, East Dereham 1916.*

Bottom left: *'D' Company team from, 32nd Battalion, The Middlesex Regiment (T.F.); winners of the bayonet fencing championship, Gorleston, December 1917.*

Top right: *A local vet and experienced hands of the men from 2/1st Derbyshire Yeomanry treating one of their mounts, East Dereham 1916.*

Bottom right: *Mills Bombing course in the entrenchments near Weybourne, winter 1917.*

built in pairs, often staggered on either side of a road on the inland side of the crossing for mutual support. The next generation of pillbox was hexagonal and made of poured concrete – these had 18 inch thick walls, half inch thick steel doors and steel lined loop holes; in many ways these pillboxes were the prototypes of what were to become the standard pillbox erected during the

There was always a great interest from the populace in the country when the military passed through the towns, see how easy it was for the Derbyshire Imperial Yeomanry to fill Norwich Street, East Dereham with their unit and onlookers in 1916.

203rd Brigade Signalling School, Great Yarmouth 1918.

Pioneer Battalion of 23rd Battalion, Royal Welsh Fusiliers in front of the Falcon Inn, Costessey 1917. Formed from Home Service personnel in 1917 this unit was part of the 224th Brigade. Stationed at Mundesley, Bacton and Hemsby they were involved in entrenchment construction and maintenance for the late war anti-invasion measures.

invasion scares of the Second World War. These hexagonal pillboxes were constructed further down the coast just outside Great Yarmouth on the Acle New Road, at Haddiscoe and St Olaves and into Suffolk. These pillboxes were built with the intention of containing an invasion force which had already landed. The army continued to rehearse procedures to combat an enemy landing as late as June 1918 and the programme of fixed emplacement construction continued cessation of hostilities when the costal defences were finally stood down and disbanded. They never fired a shot in anger but the silent sentinels of the Norfolk coast maintain their vigil; today many have been lost, are in a bad state of repair or are heavily overgrown but still they remain a reminder of the very real fears of invasion during the First World War.

Left: *An example of one of the early round pillboxes built to defend river crossings along the Ant.*

Right: *One of the 'next generation' hexagonal pillboxes near the Acle New Road.*

4 Zeppelin Raiders

'Til the day break, and the shadows flee away'
Song of Solomon 4:6 Inscribed on the grave of Flight Sub-Lieutenant John
Northrop, RNAS Great Yarmouth, killed in a flying accident 2 March 1917

Powered flight was hardly ten years old, however, its immense potential was already recognised as not only a wonder of peace time but as a weapon that could change the face of warfare forever. While Britain's Navy still ruled the waves our Coastal Type airships or 'blimps' (nick-named Pulham Pigs in these parts after the airship station near the village) were fearfully inadequate in comparison to the Germans and their advanced classes of Zeppelins which were, in effect, the long-range heavy bombers of their day. Zeppelins could cross the North Sea from their bases in the Fatherland flying far beyond the range of battleship shells or field artillery they could literally take the fight to the enemy. General von Falkenhayen, Chief of the German Army General Staff was keen to commence combined operations against Britain but his plans and airships failed to impress the Naval chiefs, they had their own plans. Admiral Hugo von Pohl, Chief of Naval staff sought an audience with the Kaiser to obtain sanction to conduct air raids on Britain. The Kaiser was initially against any such action but after conference a compromise of only allowing bombs to be dropped on specifically targeted military installations and docks was agreed; although quite how this was to be achieved on night raids with only basic navigational aids I am unsure.

On the morning of 19 January 1915 a total of three Zeppelins set out from their bases at Fuhlsbuttel and Nordholz, their mission to bombing key installations along the Humber (L.3 and L.4) and Thames Estuary (L.6). Zeppelin L.6, which had flown out of Nordholz carried no lesser man than Peter Strasser, Chief of the German Naval Airship Division; he was to "lead" the attack but their Zeppelin developed engine trouble and had to turn back, I bet he spat feathers! Zeppelins L.3 and L.4, each crewed by 16 men and armed with eight 50kg high explosive bombs and ten or eleven 28kg incendiary bombs flew out from Fuhlsbuttel under the command of Kapitanleutnant Fritz and Kapitanleutnant Magnus Count von Platen Hallermand respectively. Both airships made landfall near Bacton, L.4 turned to follow the coastline towards the West while L.3 turned south-east, where they soon even noted the Happisburgh lighthouse as their Zep passed over at about 8.00pm, shortly afterwards a patrol of the 6th (Cyclist) Battalion, The Norfolk Regiment spotted the Zeppelin as it passed over Eccles Gap.

The L.3 dropped its first bomb, an incendiary, on farmer George Humphrey's water-logged paddocks near St Michael's Church at Little Ormesby leaving only a small crater about a foot and a half wide, had turned seaward to skirt the coastline, it was then they espied Great Yarmouth and dropped a parachute flare to illuminate this target. The people below believed they were

Peter Strasser, Chief of the German Naval Airship Division.

Sketch A
Appearance of an Incendiary Bomb.

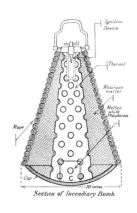

Section of Incendiary Bomb.

Norfolk Regiment
Reservists recover the
bomb dropped on
Crown Road.

Mr E. Ellis.

*Injured but undaunted
Mr Ellis stands in front
of the wrecked frontage
of his home, St Peter's
Villa.*

being swept by a searchlight and the small detachment of soldiers from the 1/6th (Cyclist) Battalion, The Norfolk Regiment who were on coastal defence duty opened up with rifle fire. Crossing the town from the south-west the L.3 dropped its second bomb, another incendiary, at 8.25pm, which landed on the back lawn of Mr N R Suffling's house at 6 Albemarle Road, overlooking the Wellesley Recreation Ground. This bomb 'burst with a loud report' but did little damage apart from gouging a two foot crater and splashing mud up the house. The third bomb, described in the *Yarmouth Mercury* as a 'diabolical thing' fell at the back of 78 Crown Road, narrowly missing one of its elderly occupants Mrs Osborne who, at the moment of impact, was crossing the small back yard to the back door; still shaking as she spoke to the reporter she said of the sound 'It was like a big gun... If I had gone just a step or two further I must have been killed by it.' On the morning after the raid this bomb was dug out of the small crater it had made in the pavement by Norfolk National Reservists, and taken to the York Road Drill Hall where the detonation mechanism was removed. The defused bomb was the object of much interest to the large number of people who came to see it through the day. The fourth bomb, an incendiary, fell a few yards further west, failing to detonate it buried itself harmlessly against the gate post of Mr W F Miller's livery stables behind Crown Road.

The people of the St Peter's Plain and Drake's Buildings area of the town were not to be so lucky. Here landed the fifth bomb, a devastating high explosive. Some of the windows of St Peter's Church and parsonage were blasted in and the front of St Peter's Villas, the home of fishworker Mr E. Ellis was brought down by the explosion. Luckily he was in the kitchen, the back door was blown off its hinges and fell on top of him, as did the kitchen window and sundry other wreckage but he only suffered cuts from flying glass and debris, and he was thankful, only minutes before he had been in the room that took the blast. He did suffer wounds severe enough to require hospital treatment, a gash to his knee caused by the falling glass penetrated deep and caused him a lot of pain. He appears on several photographs, standing indignantly in front of his house with his head bandaged.

Miss Martha Taylor.

Luckily his wife and family were away in Cornwall, where Mr Ellis was soon to join them for the mackerel fishing. Opposite the Villas were the premises of J E Pestell, builder and undertaker, that received the full force of the explosion and suffered such extensive damage they had to be demolished, he also lived on the premises with his young family, by some miracle they were all unhurt but the first casualties from the first Zeppelin air raid were incurred close by. The prostrate body of 72 year old spinster Martha Taylor who lived at 2 Drakes Buildings with her twin sister Jane Eliza was discovered outside Mr Pestell's corner office window; she had been returning from a trip to the grocers shop on Victoria Road. Miss Taylor's clothes had been blown to rags but only when she was moved was it revealed she had been badly injured in the lower part of her body and part of her arm had been blown clean off and laid nearby. A second body, that of fifty three year old shoemaker Samuel Alfred Smith was next reported. He had evidently been standing at the end of the passage in which the door of his shop was situated to watch the passing raider, the passage having a large double gate at the end, one half open and the other half closed, the bomb fell 30ft away from Mr Smith. Several fragments of the bomb blast had been hurled in his direction, the gate was badly peppered and tragically Mr Smith

Mr Samuel Alfred Smith.

The wrecked premises of J E Pestell, builder and undertaker on St Peter's Plain.

The bomb blasted windows of St Peter's Church.

was caught by some of the shrapnel, part of his head was torn away and left thigh badly horribly lacerated; found lying in a pool of blood it was clear he had stood no chance either. Other people close by were knocked off their feet by the blast, among them Mr W J Sayers and his eleven year old son Louis. They were just yards away from St Peter's Villa when the bomb went off, Mr Sayers got a 'rather nasty shaking' but his little boy received a flying fragment of glass in the shoulder. Mr Sayers said 'We went down like a pair of shot rabbits... I feel I must thank God that we are still alive. Less than 30 seconds before the bomb fell we had hurried over the very pavement it pulverised. There would not have been even enough of us for an inquest had we been slower.' William Storey and his family had recently occupied and furnished No. 17 St Peter's Plain. He had been in the kitchen with his wife their two babies, one aged two the other nine months along with his sister and a female family friend. None of them heard anything until the explosion. Mr Storey explained 'The gas went out, glass and doors flew in every direction. The women screamed but when we got a light I was relieved to find no one was hurt but we were all unrecognisable because of soot and dust.' They had a narrow escape, a large bomb fragment had 'carried the front window away' tore a hole through the stairway door and penetrated nearly two feet into the solid bricks beyond.

One notable incident was the case of Pte Poulter, a Territorial Army soldier from The Essex Regiment who was leaving the lavatory near St Peter's Church when the bomb went off and was wounded by shrapnel in the chest. It was Dr Leonard Ley who had the distinction of being the first doctor to operate on an air-raid victim. After successfully removing the piece of shrapnel he kept it and had it mounted as a tiepin, which he wore with great pride for years afterwards. The sixth and seventh bombs fell almost simultaneously, the first crashing through the roof of a stable abutting Garden Lane, near South Quay, owned by butcher William Mays. Failing to detonate, the bomb was found resting on a truss of hay beside a pony the following morning – bomb and pony both intact! This bomb was also recovered by National Reservists to the Drill Hall and an officer rendered it harmless.

The seventh bomb fell with a "huge, fiery flame", and landed opposite Messrs Woodger's shop, near the First and Last tavern on South Gates Road, near the Fish Wharf. There were no more casualties here but a number had narrow escapes. The damage was confined to a number of broken windows, lots of spattering of 'some grey substance on the walls of the houses' probably the accelerant from the incendiary and a granite paving stone was fractured by the impact. Fragments from this bomb were soon on display in the pub. The zeppelin then appears to have passed along the edge of the river dropping its ninth bomb which fell between two vessels, the drifter *Mishe Nahma* that was undergoing repairs and the pilot boat *Patrol* and striking the river side of the dock gates of Beeching's South Dock it smashed through two planks causing it to flood on the tide. The ninth bomb that fell failed to detonate and bounced off the stone quay of Trinity Wharf, narrowly missed a sentry from the National Reserve and the base of a crane turntable before it fell harmlessly into the river.

The tenth bomb fell into the 'swill' ground at the back of the Fish Wharf, blasted the water tower and made a large hole in the ground, fractured a water main and blew a nearby electric light standard to smithereens. Almost the entire glass roof of the wharf was smashed and the fish sales offices badly damaged. Several enormous chunks of the building's foundation had simply been blasted away and the refreshment rooms opposite had every window smashed – both front and back. Most of the family and staff were out and it was miraculous Miss Steel, who was in the building, playing the piano, escaped injury but was severely shaken. Two small children also had a narrow escape, they were in bed and uninjured after the blast but their covers were smothered in broken glass fragments. Miraculously, the only casualty here was Captain Smith, the Fish Wharf Master, who suffered a cut to his hand from flying glass.

The eleventh bomb was another high explosive that fell by the river blowing a hole in the quarter, 'started' the timbers and blew the rigging wire 'out like cotton' of Mr Harry Eastick's steam drifter, *Piscatorial*. It was to be his second casualty of war after he had recently lost his drifter *Copious* that sunk taking nine lives with it when struck a mine shortly after the bombardment in November 1914. This blast also damaged the maltings and a number of windows on the Southtown side.

The last bomb, the twelfth to fall during the ten minute attack, landed at the back of the racecourse grandstand on South Denes a short distance from the Auxiliary War Hospital. Leaving the largest crater of the attack, it blew down the paddock palisading, destroyed a number of fish baskets and killed a dog.

As L.3 left its devastation behind it and droned back off across the sea the L.4 was approaching King's Lynn, but let us see what had happened since the zeppelins parted after making landfall. The next reports come from Cromer as the L.4 droned low over the town local people wondered what on earth was going on, not considering the danger ran onto the streets and looked up at the raider. Most folks who saw it in Cromer agreed it was so low it almost caught

on the pinnacles of the church tower. At about 8.30 pm, when just east of Sheringham, von Platen brought the zeppelin down to 800ft and dropped a flare and soon the first bomb dropped from L.4 landed on Whitehall Yard, Wymondham Street, Sheringham. It passed through the roof, bedroom and kitchen ceiling before burying itself in the floor. The force of the landing threw a girl sat in a chair to the floor, luckily the bomb failed to detonate and no one was injured. The second incendiary fell on a building plot on Priory Road, leaving a small crater.

L.4 then turned north-west out to sea and followed the coast proceeding to drop its third bomb on the Green at Thornham, a third incendiary was

The first bomb to hit a building in the first zeppelin raid fell here at Whitehall Yard, Wyndham Street, Sheringham on 19 January 1915, luckily it did not explode.

Bomb dropped on Hunstanton by zeppelin L.4 on 19 January 1915.

dropped on the Green, before the airship headed out to sea, only to cut inland again at Brancaster, where a fourth bomb, another incendiary, was dropped near the church, about 50 yards from Dormy House and approximately 150 yards from the local auxiliary war hospital.

At Hunstanton the fifth bomb landed but did not explode near the centre of a field on the high road leading from Old Hunstanton to New Hunstanton, it was suggested in the press at the time that the zeppelin may well have been drawn by the beam of the lighthouse, in the *Report of the Intelligence Section GHQ GB on the Airship Raids from Jan to Jun 1915* states 'at 10.15 an HE bomb aimed at the wireless station dropped in a field about 300 yards away. After circling the town, which was in total darkness, it went out to sea twice, but returned each time and then made off along the coast to Heacham...'

The L.4 droned over Heacham at about 10.40 and a number of residents came onto the roads or craned their heads out of bedroom windows to look at the zeppelin as it passed overhead. Bombs six and seven were dropped here; one HE fell by Mrs Pattrick's cottage in Lord's Lane, after clipping the edge of a window sill and damaging some of the bricks in the wall, smashed part of the roof of the adjoining wash house and fell into a rain water tub – promptly blowing it to pieces – a narrow miss indeed. The second bomb did not explode and was only discovered a couple of weeks later by a lad named Dix who had been walking across Mr Brasnett's field between the council school and the chalk pit. The 1/1st Lincolnshire Yeomanry, based in Heacham at the time, dug the bomb from the ground and removed it to the lawn of 'Homemead' where the officers were staying. A sentry was posted and with the local policeman in attendance the local populace soon gathered to look at the bomb. One the Sunday an Officer drove all the way up from Woolwich Arsenal to collect the bomb and remove it for further examination, but before leaving he did confirm it was a 100lb bomb and if it had gone off would have damaged anything within a 100 yard radius.

Removed from where it was first dropped and now under guard, the people of Heacham gather on the lawn of 'Homemead' to see the bomb that had been dropped by zeppelin L.4.

Workmen boarding over the Snettisham Church windows shatterd by the bomb dropped by zeppelin L.4 on 19 January 1915.

The zeppelin continued its flight south reaching Snettisham at about 10.45. The Reverend I W Charlton, Vicar of Snettisham wrote his account of what happened next, published in the *News and County Press*: 'Supposing that the distant noise was the hum of an ordinary aeroplane, and that some lights would be visible, my wife and I and a lady friend were walking about in the garden, trying to penetrate the darkness and discover the aircraft. The drone of the engine was so much louder than usual that we were quite prepared to descry at length, exactly overhead, the outline of a Zeppelin hovering over the church and Vicarage at a great height, appearing at the distance, to be only about fifteen or twenty yards long.

No sooner had we identified it as probably a German airship, that suddenly all doubt was dispelled by a long, loud hissing sound; a confused streak of light; and a tremendous crash. The next moment was made up of apprehension, relief and mutual enquiries, and then all was dark and still, as the sound of the retiring zeppelin speedily died away.'

The zeppelin had circled the village and dropped its eighth bomb, an HE, which landed about four yards from the Sedgeford Road in Mr Coleridge's meadows causing an explosion that was felt across the village. The houses in the immediate vicinity suffered a number of broken windows, but the worst of the blast was suffered by the church. Rev. Charlton concluded 'That there was no loss of life, and that the church (with the exception of 22 windows) escaped damage, we owe, humanely speaking to the fact that the bomb fell on a soft, rain soaked meadow, with a hedge and a wall between it and the church.' After the war the windows were repaired, and the east window replaced with a stained glass 'as a thank offering for preservation and in memory of the men of this parish who fell in the Great War'.

The zeppelin then passed over Dersingham and Sandringham but dropped no bombs, however the *News and Country Press* were keen to point out the 'peculiar gusto' and 'special pleasure' of the reportage in the *Hamburger Nachricten* which claimed 'On the way to King's Lynn, Sandringham, the present residence of King George was not over looked. Bombs fell in the neighbourhood of Sandringham and loud crash notified the King of England that the Germans were not far off...Our zeppelins have shown that they could find the hidden Royal residence. In any case, they did not intend to hit it, and only gave audible notification of their presence in the immediate neighbourhood.'

L.4 approached King's Lynn from the Gaywood district and appeared the take the railway lines as its guide. Charles Hunt, the King's Lynn Chief Constable had received an unofficial report of a zeppelin raider dropping bombs on Yarmouth and Sheringham. In his report of 5 February 1915 he stated upon hearing the warning: 'I immediately communicated with the Electrical Engineer of this Borough and asked him to put the street lights out as soon as possible. He stated that his men had started putting them out and he would put further men on and get them out as soon as he could ... I at once communicated with Major Astley who is in charge of the National Guard in this town, also the Officer Commanding the Worcestershire Yeomanry who are billeted here... About 10.45pm when I was trying to get through to Dersingham the Superintendent there rang me up and stated that a Zeppelin had passed over Dersingham and had dropped Bombs in that neighbourhood. Before a message was complete I heard bombs being dropped close to this Borough. Immediately on hearing these explosions the Electrical Engineer put out all lights by switching off at the main, not only putting out lights in the streets but also in private residences as well. The Aircraft was soon over our Building and several Bomb explosions were heard almost immediately.' Immediately on the commencement of the bombardment the members of the fire brigade assembled at the station to be ready if needed, Mr G E Kendrick and the engineer were the first to arrive and they made the appliances ready.

The ninth bomb to be dropped by L.4 fell near Tennyson Avenue on a field adjoining the railway; a number of houses in the area had their windows smashed by the blast. This was followed close after by the tenth bomb which exploded 'with a grey-blue flash' on allotments that ran along the Walks side of

the railway at the Tennyson Road end, making a crater some sixteen feet across and seven feet deep and blowing in the windows of the carriages standing near the nearby railway sheds.

After droning its way menacingly over St John's Church and St James's Park the carnage really began as bomb eleven fell on Bentinck Street – a typical Victorian street, lined with poor quality terraced housing, built for working folk. It was also one of the most densely populated parts of the town and nothing short of a miracle that the casualties were as few as there were. The home of fitter's mate John Goate and his family received a direct hit, fourteen year-old Percy was killed outright, father and mother had been crushed and wounded and his four-year old sister Ethel was stunned. Mrs Goate's testimony at the inquest revealed what happened on that fateful night 'We were all upstairs in bed, me and my husband, and the baby and Percy, when I heard a buzzing noise. My husband put out the lamp and I saw a bomb drop through the skylight and strike the pillow where Percy was lying. I tried to wake him, but he was dead. Then the house fell in. I don't remember any more.'

Maud Alice Gazley, killed by the bomb dropped on Bentinck Street, 19 January 1915.

Salvaging what effects the families can from the bomb damaged houses on Bentinck Street.

The other Lynn fatality was Mrs Alice Maud Gazley a widow at just 26; her husband had been killed the previous October while serving with the Rifle Brigade at Mons. She had been sheltering with the Fayers family, neighbours of the Goate's, their house had collapsed with their neighbours after the direct hit. The Fayers all sustained minor injuries but poor Mrs Gazley had died from shock. At the inquest it was decided the injuries suffered by both Mrs Gazley and Percy Goate had been insufficient to cause their deaths and that the cause of death in both instances was shock, their death certificates both record their cause of deaths as "From the effects of the acts of the King's Enemies." Further bombs caused considerable damage on Cresswell Street and Albert Street, several people suffered minor injuries any many were treated for shock, a total of 13 people received treatment in the West Norfolk and Lynn Hospital.

The twelfth bomb exploded at the junction of Albert Avenue and East Street, at the

The spot where Percy Goate and Mrs Gazley were killed, a soldier reveals a bloodstained pillow.

back of the property owned by vet and blacksmith Mr T H Walden causing
extensive damage to the terraced houses in the area. Several people were trapped
and required assistance to get out of the rubble of their former homes.

The thirteenth bomb fell in a garden in the occupation of Mr Kerner
Greenwood at the back of his house near the docks, the bomb buried in the
garden and no severe damage was reported. Bomb fourteen fell on the power
station of the King's Lynn Docks and Railway Co. wrecking the engine house,
destroying its two boilers and the hydraulic gear that operated the Alexandra
Dock gates and caused considerable damage to surrounding buildings.

The fifteenth bomb fell on an Mr Wyatt's allotment near Cresswell Street,
causing a crater 15ft across it wrecked fences, trees and shattered windows but
luckily no-one was hurt. The final bomb of the raid, the sixteenth, fell on No.
63 Cresswell Street, the home of Mr J C Savage and his family. They all had a
lucky escape; the bomb fell through the roof crashed through the floor in the
back bedroom, through a tin box and into a basket of linen in the kitchen. It had
caused a fire to the bedroom on the way through, the fire brigade were
summoned but by the time they arrived it had been extinguished by neighbours.
The L.4 had spent its bomb load and turning seaward departed into the inky
blackness of night.

Many people suffered minor injuries caused by the flying debris and were
treated at home but a list of those who required hospital treatment was
published in the *Lynn Advertiser* viz;

    Mr Goate – cut face and swollen ankle
    Mrs Goate – Leg damaged
    Ethel Goate, aged 4 years – stunned
    Mr Fayers – cut on head
    Mrs Fayers – cut on face
    G. Hanson – back of hand cut by glass
    D. Skipper – face and head cut
    Mrs Skipper – injured leg
    G Parlett – forehead cut and head wound
    R Wykes – cut head
    R Howard – face cut in two places
    G W Clarke – cut lips
    W Anderson – wrist lacerated

In the immediate aftermath of the raids the German papers were plastered with accounts of successful attacks on fortified places between the Tyne and Humber or the 'fortified place at Yarmouth' and warnings to the King, the German crews all received Iron Crosses for their actions. The British press reflected the outrage of the British people with articles headlined 'The Coming of the Aerial Baby Killers' and reports such as *The Daily Mirror* 'Germany overjoyed by news of 'gallant' air huns murder raid' that included 'Berlin's War Whoop: Copenhagen, Jan. 20 – I have just received a private telegram from Berlin which describes the people's joy at the success of the Zeppelin attack as being widely enthusiastic. I have an intuitive feeling that the joy could not have been greater even if Dr. Barnardo's Homes had been destroyed.' The international press is typified by the New York *Tribune*, 'A Disgrace to Civilization' that spoke of a 'wanton disregard of Hague rules and humane principles. The raid belongs in the worst acts of German militarism in the present war... It is savagery which civilised opinion of the world has already condemned, which must stand condemned for all time' It was also intriguing to read in the *Daily Telegraph* the account from

the correspondent they had despatched to Lynn perhaps echoed old memories that had been stirred of the 1909 mystery airship scares by relating: 'That the hostile aircraft that attacked Lynn was guided by a pilot who was familiar with the countryside over which he flew there can be little doubt. The military and police authorities here are satisfied this is so.'

Among all the reportage after the raid one question was raised again and again – were spies at work? In Great Yarmouth the *Mercury* was quick to dismiss the stories: 'It seems a great pity that the authors of such rumours as have a disturbing effect upon the community cannot be discovered and brought to book. Many of these fairy tales concern the capture of alleged spies, and the absurd stories range from the arrest of a small crowd of Germans in an empty Howard Street shop to the detention of a young girl, a German of course, in empty business premises in the Market Place caught in the very act of flashing signals out to sea' and took particular exception to a report in another local paper that stated: 'A signal is said to have been given from Yarmouth on Tuesday evening to direct the German airship as to the best place to place bombs' and

These two images show German propaganda postcards boasting of the success of their zeppelin raids.

concluded, with some vitriol over this matter: 'We, however, feel compelled to enter a protest when the local press give publicity to such tarradiddles.'

In the west of the county questions over the presence of spies and stories such as a light being shown onto the Greyfriars Tower at Lynn or a similar account at Snettisham where 'the church spire was being constantly flashed upon' on the night of the raid were taken more seriously; above all there were accounts of a motor car that was said to have guided the zeppelin raiders to their targets with 'brilliant headlights' or 'that flashed upwards to the sky.' Mr Holcombe Ingleby, MP for King's Lynn expressed his

CITY OF NORWICH.

No. 35B. Defence of the Realm Regulations.

Bombs, &c., dropped from Hostile Aircraft; Air Raid Relics, &c.

"If any person, having found any bomb or projectile "or any fragment thereof, or any article whatsoever "which he believes or suspects to have been discharged, "dropped or lost from any aircraft or vessel of the "enemy, neglects forthwith to communicate the fact to "a military post or to a police-constable in the neigh-"bourhood, or on being so required neglects to send or "deliver the same to the competent military authority "or some person authorised by him for the purpose, he "shall be guilty of an offence against these regulations."

PENALTY.

Penalty on Summary Conviction for contravention of or non-compliance with this Regulation: imprisonment not exceeding six months, or a fine not exceeding £100, or both such imprisonment and fine.

It is of the greatest importance that the police should be immediately informed in the event of any bombs, exploded or unexploded, flares, wreckage, portions of machinery, or other articles being dropped or lost from Hostile Aircraft, and the public are earnestly requested to assist in seeing that the above regulation is strictly complied with.

Bombs should be left where they are found, as moving or handling them may cause explosions with grave risk of serious injury.

E. F. WINCH,

23rd August, 1916. *Chief Constable.*

TOWNSHEND, HARCOURT & SON, PRINTERS & ACCOUNT BOOK MANUFACTURERS, NORWICH.

The funeral cortège of Flight Sub-Lieut. G W Hillyard RNAS passes along York Road, Great Yarmouth. He had been flying a B.E. 2c on a night sortie on 8 September 1915. Despite the flares being lit on the runway, while attempting to make a landing at Bacton he landed short in an adjoining field. The undercarriage of his plane collapsed, the bombs exploded in their frames and killed the thirty year old pilot instantly. Given full military honours he buried in Great Yarmouth (Caister) Cemetery.

concerns in a letter to *The Times* published on 22 January 1915: 'I have myself tested the evidence of some of the most trustworthy of the inhabitants and the evidence seems to be worth recording. The Zeppelin is said to have been accompanied by two motor cars, one on the road to the right, the other on the road to the left. These cars occasionally sent upwards double flashes, and on one occasion these flashes from the car on the right lit up the church, on which the Zeppelin attempted to drop a bomb. Fortunately the missile fell on the grass meadow... After this attempt at wanton mischief the Zeppelin made for King's Lynn, and here again there is further evidence that it was accompanied by a car with powerful lights which were at one time directed on the Grammar School. The car was stopped in the town and attention was called to the lights as a breach of the regulations. Having put them out the driver turned the car quickly round and made off at a rapid pace for the open country. Seven bombs were dropped in King's Lynn, two of them right in the heart of the crowded streets. Possibly they were intended for more important buildings, which, without the aid of the car, it was difficult to distinguish...'

The official response to the concerns voiced by Ingleby was to dismiss the existence on the car but after Ingleby's letter and official response were also published in the local press a number of west Norfolk people wrote to him with their testimony about the mysterious signalling car. Having drawn together so many earnest accounts he brought the entire matter to the notice of the Home Secretary and published the now rare and collectable booklet *The Zeppelin Raid in West Norfolk* in 1915.

Spies or spy scares aside, Britain had been bombed and its air defences needed to be vigorously re-addressed, as Ingleby put it in the latter part of his *Times* letter 'A couple of biplanes at King's Lynn and a couple at Hunstanton might make such a raid as to which we have been subjected impossible of success. If they could not destroy a Zeppelin they might at least drive it off.' Although plans and construction work for a limited number of airfields in Norfolk, mostly for experimental aircraft, had been made in the years immediately before the First World War it took the first zeppelin raid to garner the authorities into serious active service airfield development in the county.

The extant Royal Naval Air Station at South Denes, Great Yarmouth was sent Bristol Scout 'D' aircraft specifically to conduct zeppelin patrols. Sea planes

The Orderly Room staff of the Great Yarmouth RNAS station c1917.

and flying boats were also sent to patrol the North Sea for enemy shipping. The RNAS station also had a number of satellite airfields often referred to as 'Night Landing Grounds' along and slightly inland from the coast at Narborough, Sedgeford, Holt (Bayfield), Bacton, Burgh Castle, Aldeburgh and Covehithe. In 1916-17 marker buoys were placed on Hickling Broad to provide an emergency landing place for the station's seaplanes and flying Boats.

Left: *A rare photograph of Norwich Aerodrome take by reconnaissance aircraft, June 1917.*

Right: *The Officers and men of 64 Squadron, Sedgeford 1916. Formed in August 1916 as a training unit for fighter and ground attack roles, the Squadron was deployed to active service flying out of St Omer, France in October 1917.*

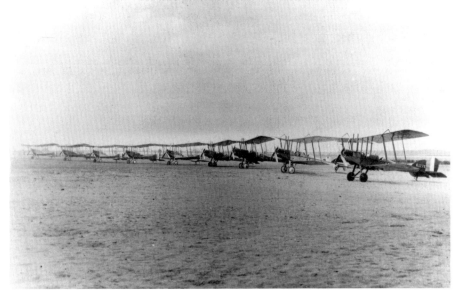

The B.E. 2e aircraft lined up at Narborough c1917.

An FE 2b from 64 Squadron after an 'up and under' at Sedgeford c1917.

Left: *Crashed Sopwith Pup, Black Dyke Feltwell c1917.*

Right: *Seaplane in the water just off RNAS Great Yarmouth.*

Henry Allingham, Europe's oldest man (at the time of writing in 2008 he is 112), and one of our Nation's last surviving servicemen of the First World War served his first posting as an Air Mechanic Second Class at RNAS Great Yarmouth. While there he was involved in the maintenance of the aircraft and took the opportunity of going flying with the pilots in the two seaters. He recalls bringing seaplanes from the water's edge up onto the slipway and how some of his comrades bitterly complained about the wading in the sea. Henry also worked at Bacton and remembers the rows of flares to mark the landing ground at night.

Henry Allingham while serving at RNAS Great Yarmouth 1915.

He remembers his station officers and many of the pilots with great affection, including Lieutenants Cadbury and Woods, especially this latter pilot whom he helped tie himself into a BE2c so he could loop the loop in it! Henry was present at Great Yarmouth on 13 April 1916 when King George inspected the Air Station and its aircraft, however, he was greatly disappointed when the King, having spoken to a number of individuals in the line of RNAS personnel assembled to meet him, turned and left just before reaching Henry's position! Later that same year Henry Allingham was sent at short notice to join the armed trawler HMT *Kingfisher*, carrying a Sopwith Schneider seaplane. *Kingfisher* was at sea during the Battle of Jutland, shadowing the British Battle Fleet. They subsequently followed the High Seas Fleet taking care to avoid the mines laid by the retreating battleships. He makes the point that the crew were not really aware that they had taken part in a major sea battle until they returned to Great Yarmouth on the Wednesday and were certainly unaware that it had been a 'victory' until the church bells rang on the Thursday. Although the trawler was not directly involved in the action, Mr Allingham can properly claim to be the last survivor of that crucial battle. Promoted to Air Mechanic First Class, he finally left Great Yarmouth in September 1917 after being posted to No 12 Squadron (RNAS) and served with them on the Western Front.

Some of the Norfolk landing grounds became airfields in their own right such as Bacton and notably Narborough that was given up by the RNAS and taken on by the Royal Flying Corps in April 1916 and grew to cover a site of some 908 acres becoming (with the exception of four airship stations), the largest aerodrome in Britain during the war. The RFC also developed airfields and landing grounds used by Norfolk based squadrons at Earsham, Freethorpe, Gooderstone Warren, Mousehold Heath, Saxthorpe, Sedgeford (taken over from RNAS by RFC in 1916 but still used as a landing field by RNAS Yarmouth until 1918), Sporle, Tottenhill, Bircham Newton, Feltwell, Harling Road, Hingham, Marham, Mattishall, Thetford and West Rudham.

A second RNAS airfield was opened in 1916 at Pulham as a naval airship base flying out mostly coastal type 'Blimps' on coastal patrols over an area that extended between a line from Margate to Dunkirk in the south and from Mablethorpe to Holland in the North. High in the air these stubby little airships were soon nick-named 'Pulham Pigs.'

Lighting restrictions had been advised across the country but before the zeppelin raid there was little response to the request; after the bombing more stringent measures were adopted, particularly in the towns affected. In King's Lynn every street lamp was extinguished by 8pm and householders required to shade their windows so no light could be seen from outside, the Lynn mart was also, under the circumstances, cancelled. In Great Yarmouth, Lowestoft and along the Norfolk coast, posters dated 24 January 1915 headed 'Defence of the Realm Regulations 1914 – Notice' and issued under the orders of Alfred A. Ellison, Captain-in-Charge, Lowestoft and Yarmouth were displayed stating 'After this date and until further notice no street lights are to be lit and all house lights as well as lights in business premises are to be screened and blinds drawn down within an area of Ten Miles from the coast from King's Lynn to Lowestoft inclusive.' Formal arrangements were made with the police across the eastern counties to provide some early warning system in the event of future raids by telephone relay system. On receipt

of such warning the electric current in the area affected would be shut off and the public required to extinguish all lights and fires. Somewhat significantly, in Lynn The Home Secretary published a notice prohibiting the use of powerful lights on motor or other vehicles, similar orders were to be repeated across the county. On 23 January 1915 six thousand handbills outlining the lighting restrictions were distributed across Norwich by Special Constables and it became an offence to show a light after dusk – even trains and trams had to draw blinds and factories working after dark had to effect a blackout over their skylights. Cyclists were not exempt and W.G. Clarke recorded in *A City in Darkness*: Until cyclists settled down to the new regulations they adopted many makeshifts, and I saw acetylene lamps with handkerchiefs tied over them, and ordinary stable lanterns with candles, laboriously fastened to the front lamp bracket.' In order to distinguish the pavements from the roadway, the kerbs in the main streets of the city were whitewashed with a spraying machine fixed to a motor tractor and what few public lights remained active were shaded and the upper part of the globes painted black. An official 'Notice to Mariners' on the East Coast was also published ordering, under the Defence of the Realm Regulations forbidding any vessels other than open boats to be under way in Great Yarmouth Roads between one hour after sunset and half an hour before sunrise, until further notice.' Lighting restrictions were soon so strict it became an offence to strike a match in the street. By the end of 1915 the stringent lighting orders had led to 1,028 summonses were dealt with by the city Justices and fines of £379. 6s had been collected.

The Royal Naval Air Service Mobile Anti-Aircraft Brigade on Yarmouth Road, North Walsham, April 1916.

Shortly after the first zeppelin raid a detachment of the The Royal Naval Air Service Mobile Anti-Aircraft Brigade was despatched under Lieutenant Mackenzie Ashton to North Norfolk with searchlights, armoured cars and high-velocity (anti-aircraft) guns. With their headquarters on Grammar School Road, North Walsham their operational area was on the north-easterly point of the county on the land behind the Happisburgh Lightship which was being used as a guide beacon by the zeppelin raiders. Following the outrage at the zeppelin raid on London the entire brigade was despatched and thus our county became the first line of land based defences for the defence of London. Commander A. Rawlinson recorded, with some pride, in *The Defence of London* 'Our column marched out of London at daylight that beautiful August morning, consisting of twelve automatic guns, three mobile searchlights and twenty other motor vehicles, including ammunition wagons and motor cycles. We carried with us ammunition, mechanical spares, telephones and all our height and range finding instruments, as well as rations; out tents and full camp equipment leaving by rail the following morning. I had the honour of leading the way and setting the pace, feeling proud indeed of our very exceptional force then under my orders, which had reached such a remarkable state of efficiency in the short space of ten months form its first inception... Keeping a nice easy speed, with the column opened out to 150 yards interval between cars to avoid the dust, we had no

mechanical trouble of any description. Having met Lieutenant Mackenzie Ashton outside North Walsham, as appointed at 1pm, we closed up the column and proceeded to the field he had obtained for us, where tents were promptly pitched and a temporary camp established. I was then able to report with a certain degree of satisfaction at 1.30pm to the Horse Guards that, having accomplished a very successful march of 150 miles, all our guns and personnel were 'present' and would be in position before dark that night. '

After food Rawlinson then 'carried on' the 5 or so miles to the coast to select and mark out gun and searchlight stations on a 20 mile front while the men obtained some rest. By night the men were in position and their own telephone communications established from each of the gun positions to Horse Guards to enable early warning of any raid. Later in the month zeppelins had made approaches across the Wash, as Rawlinson put it 'obviously searching for Sandringham House, where her Majesty Queen Alexandra was at that time in residence' so one of the detachments from the RNAS brigade, consisting of two French 75-mm auto-canons, with their ammunition wagons and searchlight, were ordered over to provide anti-aircraft defences for Sandringham. Once established, a typical active night deployment of the Headquarter Section of the RNAS Mobile Anti-Aircraft Brigade would have comprised:

Two 75-mm guns in position north of Bacton
One 3-pounder gun south of Mundesley
One 3-pounder at Watch House
One searchlight north of Mundesley
One searchlight at Walcott Gap

We must not forget another important facet of the defences of Britain in the county – high on the cliffs at Old Hunstanton, not far from the lighthouse was a secret installation colloquially known as the Hippisley Hut, and therein lies one of the stories of the country's forgotten heroes of the First World War.
Richard John Bayntun Hippisley was born in 1865 to a landed family blessed with exceptional talents in engineering and science; his grandfather had been a Fellow of the Royal Society. Bayntun, as he like to be known, began as an apprentice at the Thorn Engineering Company where he learned about mechanical and electrical engineering. He was gazetted 2nd Lieutenant in the North Somerset Yeomanry on 28 July 1888 and Honorary Lieutenant-Colonel in 1908 and was awarded the Territorial Decoration. Bayntun was an early pioneer of radio research and worked at a wireless station on the Lizard Peninsula in Cornwall where he had picked up messages from the sinking

Titanic. In 1913 he was appointed a member of the Parliamentary Commission of Wireless for the War Office Committee on Wireless Telegraphy.

Sir James Alfred Ewing (formerly the Director of Naval Education and Professor of Engineering at Cambridge) the newly appointed manager of 'Room 40', the admiralty intelligence department of cryptanalysis, was keen to obtain skilled recruits in the comparatively new field of wireless communications – and interception. In September 1914 Bayntun and barrister Edward Russell Clarke, a prominent amateur wireless expert, called at the Admiralty and informed Ewing that they were receiving messages on a lower wavelength than any being received by existing Marconi stations. The German fleet was using these low wavelengths and Ewing immediately obtained permission for Bayntun and Clarke to set up a station at Hunstanton in Norfolk. When they arrived at the coast guard station at Hunstanton they found a wooden mast with no aerial, but with a little ingenuity they were soon intercepting signals. The area around the lighthouse and across the immediate farmlands was designated a 'prohibited area,' by 1915 a maze of wireless masts stretched across the cliff top. These were controlled from within the lighthouse, which became a miniature wireless monitoring station listening in to German Navy and Airship radio traffic around the clock. Lieut Commander R J B Hippisley RNVR initially lived in the Le Strange Arms Hotel, then took over the old wooden clubhouse of the Old Hunstanton Town Golf Links and a wooden bungalow adjacent to the Cromer Road, where he installed another wireless device. The bungalow has now been replaced with brick residence but still retains the First World War *nom de guerre* of the 'Hippisley Hut.' Lieut Commander Hippisley eventually set up a string of listening posts across the British Isles and abroad. The German Navy were confident they could not be heard and never made any attempt to conceal their wireless traffic. It was these stations that picked up the unusual amount of traffic from Williamshaven that warned the Admiralty the Imperial German fleet were putting to sea before Jutland.

When the zeppelin raids intensified in 1916 fears of the wireless stations becoming a target led to the Admiralty sending a signal to say that a shallow draught monitor, HMS *Cricket* would be arriving off Hunstanton Pier. Locals recalled 'The ship had an anti-aircraft machine gun, which almost deafened the residents, and awakened the dead when it blasted off at overhead zeppelins.'

*Lieutenant Commander
R J B Hippisley RNVR*

In his article *Tradition and the innovate talent* published in *The Times* on 5 June 1995 William Rees-Mogg pointed out: 'He (Hippisley) was the man who solved the problem of listening to U-boats when they were talking to each on the radio by devising a double-tuning device which simultaneously identified the waveband and precise wavelength. That, it is said, was essential to clearing the Western Approaches in late 1917, when American troops were coming over. Bayntun Hippisley sat in Goonhilly listening to the U-boat captains as they chatted happily to each other in clear German; he told the destroyers where to find them; the food and the Americans got through.' For his services Bayntun was awarded the O.B.E. on 3 June 1918. He apparently never told his family what he did during the war and because he was bound as a gentleman, and by the Official Secrets Act,3 he did not write it down either, but suffice to say in his obituary which appeared in *The Times* on 11 April 1956, Bayntun was described as 'an almost unique personality' who 'inherited a remarkable mechanical and scientific gift, which put him in the forefront, if not ahead, of most of his contemporaries.' One of the senior officers who had worked with Bayntun remarked that Hippisley 'was one of the men who really won the war'.

As an example of the work and worth of the Admiralty interceptor station at Hunstanton consider the afternoon of 2 September 1916 when they intercepted a coded message from a zeppelin and relayed by telephone to the cryptographers at the Admiralty. Once deciphered it was established that sixteen airships, of the German Army and Navy were mounting a combined attack (all sixteen started but only twelve actually made landfall, the target, although not obtained from the radio traffic, came as no surpise – it was London). Armed with the intercepted information at 8.15pm GHQ Home Forces were able to order 'Extra vigilance.' At 9.15pm GHQ ordered the RNAS Mobile Anti-Aircraft Brigade 'Take air raid action' and soon afterwards the first two zeppelins were seen approaching and then hovering over the Haisboro Lightship where they waited and allowed the other airships to catch up they then moved off and made landfall. The first bombs fell near the RNAS airfield at Bacton and bombs were heard falling around the area. The searchlights swept the sky for the attackers but visibility was poor and they could only occasionally pick out the airships in brief moments of broken cloud, Commander Rawlinson recorded in the RNAS Mobile AA Brigade log: 'it was impossible to hold the target in the beam. No. 1 gun did not bear (dead angle); fired five rounds from No. 2 gun at target.' More zeppelins could be heard passing over but still the RNAS Brigade were frustrated, the log continues 'Aircraft heard approaching from SW. Weather thick, clouds low. Crossed coast over Bacton 3-pounder gun, 1 Mile south of headquarters. The airship was momentarily visible to the naked eye through rifts in clouds at intervals at from 6,000 to 8,000 feet altitude. The 75-mm section fired eleven rounds from No. 1 gun, seven rounds from No. 2 gun, range 4,000 to 6,500 yards, altitude 6,000 to 8,000 feet, gradually rising. Very few of the bursts could be observed owing to clouds, which also rendered the searchlights of no value. This target was visible to the Mundesley gun, but out of range of it... the Bacton gun, near whose position it passed the coast was only able to fire one round at 8,000 feet altitude. Ten bombs were dropped before passing the coast, some falling at Ridlington Common, less than one mile from Bacton 3-pounder gun position and close to Bacton Naval Aerodrome where flares were burning and whose aeroplanes were 'up.'' Although the brave boys of the RNAS on land and in the air were courageously 'doing their bit' history will record the night as belonging to the Royal Flying Corps. No.39 Squadron went up from Sutton's Farm near Hornchurch, Essex at eleven o'clock, among them Lieutenant William Leefe Robinson in his converted B.E. 2c. night fighter. The drums of his machine guns were loaded with the brand new Brock-Pomeroy mixed incendiary ammunition that could puncture the envelope and gas cells of the airship, releasing the hydrogen and ignite it with the phosphorous bullet. On this patrol, on this night Leefe Robinson was to become the first man to shoot down an airship over Britain – the SL.11 that came down in a ball of fire at Cuffley. Robinson was awarded the Victoria Cross and German confidence of mastering the air with their zeppelins was literally shot down in flames. The largest air raid of all time had been foiled and having shown a biplane, armed with the right sort of ammunition, could shoot down an airship; it was to prove the beginning of the end for the 'zeppelin menace.'

Although the Germans had received a knock from the downing of airship SL.11 air raids continued, through the war it was recorded that on sixty occasions 'air raid action' was taken in the Norwich and numerous additional alerts. More bombs were dropped across Norfolk, not as part of raids targeting places in the county but as the airships swept over the county to and

W. E. Johns, the creator of Biggles had been the assistant sanitary surveyor of Swaffham before war broke out. He had joined the Norfolk Yeomanry and served with them in Gallipoli. Always in search of adventure he transferred to The Machine Gun Corps and volunteered when the call came for pilots in the Royal Flying Corps and flew out from Norfolk airfields on a number of occasions before he left for France to serve in a night bomber squadron.

Left: *The view down Church Street, East Dereham, after the raid on the evening of of Wednesday 8 September 1915.*

Right: *Damaged houses and business premises on Church Street, the severely damaged White Lion is on the right.*

from raids on other parts of the country, predominantly London. The bombs dropped on our county in these instances rarely caused serious damage although Ridlington church did have its chancel blown in and still the brave soldiers of the National Reserve dealt with most of the unexploded devices. The last serious raid on the county during the First World War occurred shortly before 9pm on Wednesday 9 September 1915 when zeppelin L.14 under the command of Kapitänleutnant Alois Böcker bombed East Dereham.

The zeppelin swept over the town from the direction of Scarning. The first four bombs dropped on Church Farm meadows causing little more damage than blasting a gate by a barley stack and blowing the leaves off a hedge but it did cause the patients in the War Hospital to run out and investigate in their night attire. The next three bombs landed on marshy meadows blowing out stinky black mud over a large area. The next bombs were increasingly serious; landing on the roadway near Dereham Guildhall leaving a crater 6ft across and 4ft deep bringing down part of the Guildhall outbuildings, badly damaged the roof of the infant school on the opposite side of the road and smashed some of the glass in the church windows. The worst damage was caused by the bombs dropped on Church Street. The premises of H H Aldiss's shop on the High Street corner was nearly wrecked, the windows of the King's Arms and Cave's photographers were blasted in, the White Lion pub was so badly damaged it never opened again and two patrons, Mr Harry and Mrs Sylvia Johnson were badly injured. In this upper area of the street the body of L/Cpl Alfred Pomeroy was found, his left leg, abdomen and pelvis horribly mangled from the blast, parts of his body were

Wrecked cottages in White Lion Yard.

found on the roof of a building next to the Corn Hall. Mr James Taylor was passing along the top of Church Street to post a letter when the bomb landed. His body was found lying in the road near the National Provincial Bank 'shot in the abdomen by a piece of shell case.' The frontage of Hamerton's grocery shop was blown out and cottages in White Lion Yard were badly damaged, one of them collapsing on top of its occupants, Mr and Mrs Taylor. On the opposite side of the road many houses were scarred by the flying shrapnel and the orderly rooms of 5th Battalion, The Norfolk Regiment had its windows shattered and roof smashed. The body of Harry Patterson was found in the entrance of the 5th Norfolk's headquarters, a piece of steel shell casing having penetrated his chest.

The Corn Hall had its glass roof smashed and a bomb fell on a nearby house demolishing it. The occupant, Mr Catton had heard the commotion outside and ran out to investigate as a soldier ran inside to take shelter – he was extracted alive from the collapsed building but died later from his injuries. The bank also had their windows smashed along with the Alexander family memorial windows in the Cowper Memorial Church. The zeppelin then swept away towards Bayfield Hall, leaving a trail of bombs along the way, most of which fell on farm and estate land. But then, ominously, the zeppelin turned again and made another pass over Dereham. On this second run an incendiary was dropped on Bradley's ironmongers in the Market Place, setting fire to the oil store and adjacent cartridge store which began exploding the ammunition in the intense heat. Terry Davy in *Dereham in the Great War* recorded what happened next 'The fire brigade is summoned by the firing of maroons, and immediately the fire broke out at Bradley's, Mr Herbert Leech, who had a men's outfitting business at the other end of the Market Place, ran to the King's Arms Hotel where the maroons are kept. He found all the occupants down the cellar and, as bombs were falling rapidly, nobody answered his request for the maroons to be fired. Eventually he was given the key to the outbuilding where the maroons were kept. Mr Leech enlisted the assistance of a passing soldier and they got the maroons out. He knew nothing about firing them and actually

Repairing the bomb damage to the 5th Battalion, The Norfolk Regiment Headquarters on Church Street.

The view across Dereham Market Place to the houses near the Corn Hall that recived a direct hit and killed a soldier sheltering inside.

held the match in his hand whilst lighting the fuse! When the first maroon was fired the soldier rolled over amongst the cabbages in the garden and bolted! Mr Leech fired the second maroon as the Zeppelin was hanging directly over head and it immediately fled. The Zeppelin's departure was attributed by many to Mr Leech's courage and for this he has been complimented by military officers and prominent people of the town.'

The casualties were listed as:

Killed

> James Taylor (61) an Earthenware, China and General dealer, 27 High Street, Dereham
> Harry Patterson (44), watchmaker and jeweller, High Street, Dereham
> Lance Corporal Alfred Edward Pomeroy 2/1st City of London Yeomanry (Rough Riders)

Died of Wounds

> Pte Leslie Frank McDonald 2/1st City of London Yeomanry (Rough Riders)
> Pte H G Parkinson 2/1st City of London Yeomanry (Rough Riders)

Injured

> Mr and Mrs Johnson, Baxter's Row, Dereham – Wounded by shrapnel
> Mr and Mrs Taylor, White Lion Yard, Dereham – Injured by house collapsing on them
> Miss Dawson, Scarning Fen – Injury to ankle
> Pte A W Quinton London Mounted Brigade Field Ambulance RAMC – Wounded in leg.

The history of Norfolk has been filled with many significant firsts and lasts, the First World War was no exception. The first zeppelin raid on Britain happened here, as we have seen in this chapter, on 19 January 1915 and the very last zeppelin to be shot down also occurred here on 5 August 1918. Fregattenkapitan Peter Strasser, Head of the German Naval Airship Division (the man who would have led the first zeppelin raid personally had the airship carrying him not developed mechanical problems and had to turn back) was aboard the LZ 112 (L.70) as his 'flagship' to lead an attack on London. A total of five airships were to carry out the raid, three of them the L.53, L.65 and L.70, with Strasser on board chose to make their approach over the East Coast. On that light evening, at 8.10pm the three zeppelins were sighted by lightships 30 miles north-east of Happisburgh. Messages were relayed across the sea until the East Coast defences were alerted. The telephone of the Great Yarmouth RNAS station rang with the warning and the Duty Officer, Captain Robert Leckie commander of 228 Squadron, the 'Boat Flight' acted immediately. Informing the station commander, Lt. Col. Nicholl, orderlies were sent post haste across the town to call in officers and men, including Temporary Major Egbert Cadbury, commander of 212 Squadron from Wellington Pier where he had been attending a charity concert. At the cinema, the film clattered to a stop and the glass lantern slide projected on the screen stating: 'All officers wanted at Air Station immediately.' Rushing back on foot, bicycle or bundling onto the station's ford tender the aircrew and pilots knew the drill and soon thirteen aircraft; DH-4s, DH-9s and Sopwith Camels, were in the air from Great Yarmouth, Burgh Castle and Covehithe, with twenty more soon joining them in the air over the county from airfields farther inland. Station Duty Officer Leckie turned over the station to its permanent commander and jumped in the rear or observer-gunner seat behind Cadbury in a DH-4 as its 375-hp Rolls-Royce Eagle warmed up. Both

Cadbury and Leckie were seasoned in zeppelin combat, both had already shot down airships and had been recognised for their gallantry.

Once over the sea, in an attempt to increase his rate of climb Cadbury ditched the two 100-pound bombs used against surface craft that had been fitted to the DH-4's rack. This appeared to make little or no difference; Cadbury put it down to the barometric pressure. At 9pm Strasser sent a final Morse code message to his command: 'To all airships, attack according to plan from Karl 727. Wind at 5,000 meters [16,250 feet] west-southwest three doms [13.5 mph]. Leader of airships.'

Major Cadbury recorded: Immediately on leaving Yarmouth I sighted 3 zeppelin airships to north-east, distant about 40 miles, steering west at a slow speed, and I gave chase... At approximately 21.45 the Zeppelins, which were flying in vee-formation, altered course north, at 22.10 Zeppelin abeam 2,000 feet above us at 17,000 feet. At 22.00 we had climbed to 16,400 feet and I attacked the Zeppelin ahead slightly to port so as to clear any obstruction that might be suspended from the airship. My observer [Captain Leckie] trained his gun on the bow of the airship and the fire was seen to concentrate on a shot under the Zeppelin, three-quarters way aft... The Z.P.T. [the phosphorous bullets] was seen to blow a great hole in the fabric and a fire started which quickly ran along the entire length of the zeppelin. The zeppelin raised her bows as if in an effort to escape, then plunged seaward, a blazing mass. The airship was completely consumed in about three quarters of a minute. Captain Freudenreich, commander of the nearby L.63 stated later: 'I was nearing the coast when we suddenly saw an outbreak of flame on the L.70, amidships or a little aft. Then the whole ship was on fire. One could see flames all over her. It looked like a huge sun. Then she stood up erect and went down like a burning shaft. The whole thing lasted thirty, maybe forty-five seconds.' Cadbury and Leckie pursued the other zeppelins, further hits were achieved but due to their high altitude, a gun jam and increasingly cold conditions (in the rush to leave Yarmouth Leckie had forgotten his gauntlets) the zeppelins got away into the now dark and rainy night. Cadbury and Leckie were a long way from their base at Yarmouth but sighting the flares of Sedgeford landed there at 11.05 p.m. It was only when he jumped down from the cockpit that Cadbury realized why the DH-4 had climbed so sluggishly. The two bombs that he thought he had released

Major Egbert Cadbury DSC DFC and Captain Robert Leckie DSO DSC DFC photographed at RNAS Great Yarmouth a few hours after they shot down zeppelin L70.

GERMAN BOMB

One of the unexploded bombs, weighing 110lbs with Barbara Gower (3) left and Margaret Kemp (nearly 4) on the right.

LIVE BOMB
DUG BY
PC.T BULLEN
N.S

The brave men of the Norfolk National Reserve shortly after digging out another bomb, dropped on Coltishall during the last air raid 1918.

into the sea were still in place, *and primed*, but by some miracle still intact despite a rough landing. Just one more jolt and the DH-4 could well have been blown to pieces! Later, both Cadbury and Leckie were recognised for their action with the award of the Distinguished Flying Cross.

The L.70 came down about 8 miles just north of Wells-next-the-Sea, close to the schooner *Amethyst*. A search of the sea soon revealed neither Strasser nor any of his 22 crew had survived. The British military authorities did not wait for the sea to give up its dead. Within two days a trawler in naval service had located and buoyed the wreckage of L.70. Over the following three weeks much of the wreck was recovered by divers and wire drags. From this watery grave came code books and all manner of airship intelligence, the body of Strasser and a number of his crew were also found, a number were also washed up on the nearby coastline. All were buried at sea and with them the future of the German military airship in modern warfare.

Postscript: The end of the zeppelin menace did not end the German attacks on Norfolk. At 10.55pm on Monday 14 January 1918, Great Yarmouth was again shelled by German warships. This time some shells did hit their mark, houses and buildings were damaged, windows were blown in, there were many lucky escapes but eight people were injured and four killed. Able Seaman Thomas Prigent (42) and ship's fireman John Simpson (17) were asleep on board their vessel in the harbour when the shell struck the forecastle deck. Both were recovered and rushed to hospital but later died of their wounds. Mr Alfred Sparks (53) and his wife Mary Ann (53) were also asleep when a shell struck their bedroom. Mrs Sparks had been killed instantly but Alfred was dug out of the rubble and removed to the hospital where he died from his wounds shortly after 10am the following morning.

5 For King and Country

They went with songs to the battle, they were young,
Straight of limb, true of eye, steady and aglow.
They were staunch to the end against odds uncounted;
They fell with their faces to the foe.

From 'For the Fallen', Laurence Binyon (1914)

A brief overview of the Battalions, major actions and fighting men of The Norfolk Regiment 1914-1918

Regular Army Battalions

1st Battalion

Mobilized for war from Holywood, Belfast and after being brought back up to war service strength by reservists formed part of the 15th Brigade, 5th Division British Expeditionary Force (BEF). They landed at Le Havre and entrained for the front on the night of 17 August 1914 and arrived at Le Cateau the following day. The battalion fought at Mons (Elouges), Le Cateau, the Aisne, La Bassee

Regular soldiers of the 1st Battalion, The Norfolk Regiment on the eve of war 1914.

and Ypres. Christmas 1914 was spent in the trenches near Ploegsteert (Plug Street to the Tommies). The weather was vile, frost and snow frequent; the men were exposed to varying depths of water and mud and trench foot became prevalent. On Christmas Day the men of the 1st Battalion were present at the famous 'Christmas Truce.' Cromer man, Lance Corporal Walter Balls of B Company wrote his experiences of the day to his old friend Roy Read who published the letter in the *Norfolk Chronicle*: On Christmas Day things were very quiet. I don't think there was a rifle shot on either side near us. At night we could hear them singing in the trenches quite plain, so we got a good fire up and did ditto – carols and songs, A1. I should have told you that every night we slip across the field to a farm and get enough water to last til the next night. On Boxing morning we could see the Germans on top of their trenches walking about. So we did ditto. Some of them came across so some of us went half way

81

The men of 1st Battalion, The Norfolk Regiment in the trenches near 'Plug Street' Christmas 1914.

Pte Arthur Lewis Alcock, 1st Battalion, The Norfolk Regiment. Son of Mr. G. W. and Mrs. E. Alcock, of The Building, Syderstone, King's Lynn. Killed in action 28 October 1917. He was 23.

to meet them and shake hands with them. One could speak English well. He told us they did not want to fight. One of the officers snapped one of our chaps with a small camera. He told us they were the 45th and 49th regiments and they fought with us at — and —; they were "driven to the firing line" to use his own words "death in front and death behind". They were going back to a concert. After that I had a look around the farm. It was tobacco on half of the field and potatoes the other half. About a dozen bullocks etc laid about the field killed, we buried them later. On Christmas Day we had photos of the King and Queen from them and Princess Mary pipe tobacco and fags. I shall send them home if I can.'

At the end of February 1915, 15 Brigade was moved from the neighbourhood of Messines to the southern face of the Ypres salient and the notorious 'Hill 60', it was a time to take stock, and it was by this time of the officers who had left Belfast in August 1914 only five of them remained in the battalion. Over the ensuing months of holding the lines, raids and attacks the casualties were so frequent the men of the battalion stoically became all too familiar with losing their comrades or seeing another pal removed to the aid post. In May 1915 the battalion suffered one of the first gas attacks on the western from and suffered 75 casualties from it on 5 May 1915. The battalion were relieved the following day after 26 days continuously in the trenches. After a brief time to recuperate and reinforce the 1st Battalion was returned to the lines of the Albert Front. From September to December 1915 the battalion's front trench service was in the area between Carnoy and Mametz. The increasing challenge for the men, on top of the fighting, was the terrain which after a year of pounding by artillery, bombs and mines now resembled more of the moon than Northern France. Liquid mud and water filled the craters and if a shell or mine blew nearby, if the blast did not injure or kill, men could easily become buried under the earth displaced by the explosion and there are numerous incidents involving officers, NCOs, men and particularly the stretcher bearers digging out men who had become buried, they also helped the men involved in tunnelling and mining. Often such rescues were, by necessity of the men soon losing oxygen, conducted under fire such as on 1 December 1915. The battalion had just got into the trenches near Mametz when the Germans exploded a mine in the sector, causing several casualties among the mining and tunnelling fatigues. In rescuing buried men, gallant service was done by Lieutenant Burlington, Sergeant Dunrabbin and Private Doughty. For this the Officer received the MC and the others the DCM. Pte R G Doughty's citation points out he: 'volunteered to be lowered down the shaft and brought an unconscious man to the surface. The air was foul with gas fumes but he remained a long time helping to rescue others.'

In July 1916 the men of 1 Norfolk served with distinction in action to capture Longueval High Wood and Delville Wood but it was to cost them the lives of 17 officers and 412 other ranks in the space of a week. Over the ensuing months they fought again at Falfemont Farm, Morval and Givenchy. On 1 October 1916 the battalion left the Somme area, but not without a special battalion order from the Commanding Officer, Colonel Stone

'Before leaving the Somme and all it will mean to us and to the history of the Regiment, I wish to convey my most sincere thanks to all ranks for what they have done... You had everything against you, but you have been through the heaviest fighting of the war and come out of it with a name that will live forever.

At Longueval, your first battle you were given your first and severest test, and no praise of mine can be too high for the extreme gallantry and endurance shown on that occasion. The severest test of discipline is for men to stand intense shell fire and to hold on to the ground they have won under it – and this you did. At Falfemont Farm you again had a difficult task and a severe fight, but you stuck to it and eventually captured it, a position whose importance cannot be over-estimated. Then, during the most trying weather conditions, you were in the open making trenches and at one time the limit of complete exhaustion had almost been reached, but when one final effort was asked of you at Morval, you carried out a brilliant assault... You came to the Somme battle-field with a very high reputation, which you had rightly earned during twenty-three months of strenuous warfare – you leave the Somme with the highest reputation in the British Army.'

And so the men of the 1st Battalion fought on into 1917 through Vimy, Oppy Wood and back again to Ypres in the Battle of Cambrai. But then came the great Austro-German offensive on the Italian Front which saw seven French and five British divisions sent to reinvigorate the Italian Army. The men of the 1 Norfolk were despatched in November 1917 and were undoubtedly pleased to get out of the trenches of the Western Front. They were not unduly taxed by their role in the lines around Piave and their sojourn would not be for long and they returned to the Western Front in April 1918. Within days they were in the advance guard of the brigade to St Venant, south of the key battle area of Nieppe Forest, where again the men fought with distinction. In July the curtain was raised on the last 'Big Push' and by August 5th Division was attached to 4th Corps. These final battles of the war were hard won for the men of the 1st Battalion, many of the stalwarts of the battalion who had been with them through thick and thin over the last few years fell at this last hurdle, many to wounds sustained under the intense German shell fire, among them the CO, Lieut-Colonel Humphries, Captain G C Tyler the adjutant and even Rev. R W Dugdale MC CF, the padre was killed. But the battalion came through with laurels, the Divisional Commander formally asked their CO to inform all ranks 'how much he appreciated the extraordinary good work carried out by the battalion during the operations from 21 August to 2 September.' The men of the 1st Battalion entered their last action of the war at 5.30am on 5 November when they led an attack on the forest of Mormal from Neuville. Withdrawn to Jolimetz on the west of Mormal Forest it was here news was received of the Armistice on 11 November 1918.

2nd Battalion

August 1914, in Belgaum, India, sent as part of 18th Indian Brigade, 6th (Poona) Division to Mesopotamia in November 1914. They did see action in 1914 and had experience of using their bayonets in the attack on Kurna, they saw out 1914 on the banks of the River Tigris but their first major action was to be one which was to be etched bold among the most notable in the history of the Regiment. On 14 April 1915 2 Norfolk received the order 'Push forward at all costs. Take the enemy's trench.' Colonel Peebles drew his sword and in the finest traditions of the Norfolk Regiment led the attack personally with the shout of 'Come on the 9th!' attacked an estimated enemy force of some 10,000 to 12,000 Turks in heavily wired trenches, redoubts and well made gun emplacements at Shaiba. As Tim Carew described it in *The Royal Norfolk Regiment*: ...they advanced over 500 yards of featureless desert and never a man faltered –

Second Lieutenant Harry Norton Fox of Hickling, killed in action while serving with 1st Battalion, The Norfolk Regiment at La Coulotte near Lens, 23 April 1917. He has no known grave but is com-memorated on the Arras Memorial. He was 23.

Captain Terence Algernon Kilbee Cubitt MC, 1st Battalion, The Norfolk Regiment, killed in action on the final advance, Achiet le Petit on 22 August 1918.

One of the smart Regular soldiers of the 2nd Battalion, The Norfolk Regiment, Belgaum, India 1914.

Men of the 2nd Battalion, The Norfolk Regiment, near Ctesiphon, Mesopotamia 1915.

machine gun and rifle bullets zipped about their ears, but still they came on. They charged, heedless of fire and casualties, yelling as men will, to keep their hearts jumping out of their mouths; the Turks, shaken by the wildness of the charge, fled from them, and the mile long low ridge which was the Shaiba position became the property of the 2nd Battalion, The Norfolk Regiment.'

Such was this victory the men of the 2nd Battalion, and indeed the regiment have celebrated 'Shaiba Day' ever since. It was a decisive victory and one of the last occasions when British Army officers carried swords in action but many men fell on that desert soil, there was the wounded and sickness took its toll on the men too; by the following day Major de Grey estimated they were left with about 300 men. As 1915 rolled on heatstroke and diseases like beri-beri and dysentery claimed many of the men. Their next major action was at the Battle of Ctesiphon in October 1915. The battalion fought with just 500 men after which just seven officers and 250 men were left on their feet. And then those left were sent to Kut-al-Amara; here they spent the Christmas of 1915, under siege in the stinking and oppressive environs of Kut. The rations were soon depleted and men were reduced to ten ounces of bread and one pound of horse or mule flesh. Amidst such deprivation the men of 2 Norfolk did not waver, General Townshend wrote in his despatch 'It is my handful of Norfolks, Dorsets and Oxfords who are my sheet anchor here.' But despite their solid will their bodies were weakened through starvation and disease. On 29 April 1916, after 146 days of siege, Kut was surrendered and the remnants of the 2nd Battalion there became prisoners of war. But that was not to be the end of the 2nd Battalion – there were still available drafts and recovered sick or wounded of the Norfolk and Dorset Regiments. Neither regiment had enough men to raise a battalion in their own right so on 4 February 1916 it was decided to take two companies from each and raise a composite battalion, soon known to the men as 'Norsets.' They fought at Sannaiyat and despite outbreaks of cholera held their positions along the Tigris until the 2nd Battalion was reconstituted in July at Basra. Few of these men were 'old soldiers,' the majority of the new men coming equally from Kitchener and Derby recruit schemes. They returned to the Tigris and over

Men of 2nd Battalion, The Norfolk Regiment blindfolding a Turkish prisoner before conducting him through British lines, Jebel Hamarin 1918.

the next two years drove the Turks back along its course transferring in February 1917 to 37th Indian Brigade, 14th Indian Division. When Lieut-General Sir R G Egerton relinquished command of the 3rd (Indian) Corps he communicated his appreciation of 2 Norfolk in these later actions: 'The great feat of arms performed by you in the clearance of the Dahra Bend was followed by the magnificent achievement at Shumran, when you forced the passage of the Tigris in full flood in the face of a determined enemy – a performance, which will, I believe, live in history as unique in the annals of any army in the world. And in connexion with this I raise my hand to salute the gallant Norfolk Regiment in particular.'

Twenty two year old Pte Bernard William Childs of Swafield, who died while serving with 2nd Battalion, The Norfolk Regiment in Mesopotamia on 22 May 1916.

Troops of 2nd Battalion, The Norfolk Regiment with sentry/lookout posted, Lewis gun and rifles in position the guard a barren outpost on the, Jebel Hamarin 1918.

Soldiers of The Norfolk National Reserve c1915.

3rd (Special Reserve) Battalion

Initially based at Britannia Barracks as a training and depot unit. On Saturday 8 August the battalion was despatched to Felixstowe forming part of the Harwich Garrison coastal defences where it remained for the rest of the war. In addition the 3rd Battalion acted as the conduit for many Militiamen, Reservists and unattached Officers before they joined battalions on 'Active Service' as well as training and despatching drafts overseas. A tragedy recalled by the Commanding Officer Colonel Tonge was the loss of the troop transport ship *Royal Edward* after being torpedoed Aegean Sea in August 1915. Of the 1,400 men she carried only 600 were saved. Out of these all but 18 of 300 men who had volunteered from the battalion to serve in The Essex Regiment survived. In July 1919 the battalion was despatched to Ireland on peace keeping duties. The battalion was were eventually absorbed by 1st Battalion.

Territorial Force

When the winds of war blew in 1914 the War Office knew that Territorial soldiers were under no obligation to fight overseas but knowing the 'call may come' a general appeal was put out to the Territorial battalions for volunteers for overseas service. The response was very positive, with many Territorial battalions sending in returns of around 90% volunteering 'to do their bit overseas.' A white metal pin backed badge bearing the legend 'Imperial Service' surmounted by a crown was issued to those who volunteered before 30 September 1914, and was worn with great pride above the right pocket on the tunic. Very few Territorial units were to see action in the opening battles of The First World War like Mons or the Marne. In fact many were tasked with the duties for which they were originally raised – guarding the homeland with our Territorial cyclist battalions deployed in patrolling and maintaining coastal defences thus providing the 'first line' in the event of an invasion.

New recruits for the Territorials of 4th Battalion, The Norfolk Regiment on the march in Norwich 1914.

1/4th Battalion

Mobilized at Drill Hall on Chapel Field, Norwich, part of the Norfolk and Suffolk Brigade, East Anglian Division, the battalion officially became part of the 163rd Brigade, 54th Division in May 1915. They landed at Suvla Bay, on 10 August 1915 and served throughout Gallipoli Campaign. In December 1915 their division was sent to the Middle East; landing at Alexandria the battalion spent the rest of war in Egypt and Palestine; and served with distinction with the 5th Battalion at the Second Battle of Gaza in April 1917.

2/4th (Reserve) Battalion

Formed at the Chapel Field Drill Hall, Norwich in August 1914 as a second line battalion, its purpose was to supply drafts for overseas units and continue recruiting for the battalion to enable it to undertake Home Defence. On the formation of the East Anglian Division TF it was the first to complete its establishment and moved to divisional headquarters at Peterborough in November 1914. Moved to Lowestoft in January 1915 they undertook the construction of defences for the port, provided personnel for naval searchlights and helped man the No. 2 Armoured Train. They remained on duty at locations along

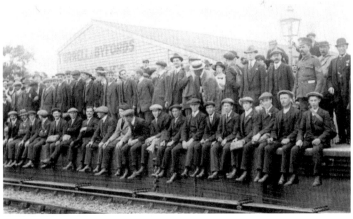

Volunteers from Attleborough leaving from the station 1914.

the Suffolk coast until November 1916 when re-named 11th Battalion, Norfolk Regiment T.F. In December 1916 the battalion was transferred to the 212th Brigade, 71st Division and moved to Aldershot command, stationed at Guildford. Moved to Colchester in March 1917 the category A and B1 men were transferred to overseas unit, the unit was gradually wound down and finally disbanded by order of the Army Council in July 1917.

1/5th Battalion

Mobilized at their HQ in East Dereham the battalion officially became part of the 163rd Brigade 54th Division in May 1915. They landed at Suvla Bay 10 August 1915. On 12 August 1915 the battalion was involved in an attack at

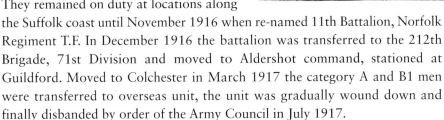

Norfolk Regiment soldiers on route march 1915.

Pte Geoffrey John Griston, one of the 1/5th Battalion, The Norfolk Regiment posted 'Missing' during the infamous attack at Kuchuk Annafarta Ova, Gallipoli, 12 August 1915. He has no known grave but is commemorated on the Helles Memorial.

Kuchuk Annafarta Ova, the battalion pushed as far as they could but became fragmented and the farthest forward soldiers penetrated enemy lines, the enemy closed in and the battalion suffered terrible casualties of 22 officers and 350 men (figures according to the War Diary). The King had a personal interest in the battalion, men from his estate at Sandringham were serving in the officer corps, among the NCOs and in the ranks and his friend and Estate Agent, Frank Beck, was a Company Commander. At the time the dead from the forward troops of the battalion were now behind enemy lines and not knowing if the men were killed or taken prisoner many families were simply notified that their relative was 'Missing.' The King pressed for information but specifics, at the time, could not be given. Sir Ian Hamilton's despatch, worded with his flowery prose, describes 'a very mysterious thing' where 'the colonel, sixteen officers and 250 men, still kept pushing on, driving the enemy before them... Nothing more was ever seen or heard of any of them. They charged into a forest and were lost to sight or sound. Not one of them ever came back.' The bodies of the 5th Battalion soldiers who fell on that day were discovered by the Graves Registration Unit in September 1919, sadly most were beyond individual identification but the damage was done and the 'mystery' of the disappearing Norfolks had entered into military myth, much in the style of the 'Angel of Mons' and has been discussed in serious and scurrilous publications ever since. In December 1915 their division was sent to the Middle East; landing at Alexandria the battalion spent the rest of war in Egypt and Palestine and served with distinction with the 4th Battalion at the Second Battle of Gaza in April 1917.

New recruits for 2/5th Battalion, The Norfolk Regiment on parade in East Dereham Market Place 1914.

2/5th Battalion

Under the expansion scheme of the Territorial Force a Reserve Battalion of 5 Norfolk was raised in East Dereham, at the HQ of the 1/5th Battalion in October 1914 initially known as 5th (Reserve) Battalion, The Norfolk Regiment (T.F)

Although they had no uniforms, rifles or equipment, their zeal in drill, exercise and training were 'remarkable' and their fine, uniformed band under Bandmaster Dines was a

great asset. But the uniform situation for the men became critical to the development of the unit. Sir Aylwin Fellows, the Chairman of the Norfolk Territorial Force Association visited the HQ and upon seeing for himself gave leave for the OC to buy boots and what uniform could be procured for the troops – and the association would pay the bills. The only khaki uniforms and most of the greatcoats which could be procured were second hand and even with those procured when the battalion was ordered to proceed to Peterborough on 5 December 1914 a number of men still had to march with their comrades wearing their civvy coats and caps.

Men of 2/5th Battalion, The Norfolk Regiment marching in to Peterborough. Few had a full uniform but their spirits were high.

In early January 1915 a fully uniformed recruiting march was staged across the principal towns of Norfolk by the band and a hand-picked cadre of men under two or three officers and NCOs. The result was a fine body of recruits that brought the battalion up to strength and organised into four strong companies under Captains T B Hall, G. J. Bracey, H. Smith and H A Durrant.

The Battalion was quartered in Peterborough until May 1915 when it proceeded to Cambridge and marched to Bury St Edmunds in late July 1915 and after five days there moved to camp at Thetford. In August 1915 the Battalion moved to undertake trench construction for the defence of London scheme at

Brentwood in Essex. While in Brentwood many of the junior officers left the 2/5th to join the active service battalions shortly before they departed for Gallipoli. By winter the remainder of 2/5th had returned to Bury and were eventually absorbed into 4th (Reserve) Battalion.

3/4th and 3/5th Battalions

Formed in early 1915 at Norwich and East Dereham respectively. Both battalions were quartered in their 'Home' depot city and town until August 1915 when they were moved to Windsor Great Park. In the first week of October 1915 they moved again to Halton Camp near Tring in Hertfordshire and from there both battalions sent out many drafts to the 1/4th and 1/5th Battalions in the Middle East.

In February 1916 the battalions were formally designated 4th and 5th (Reserve) Battalions. On 1 September 1916 the 4th Battalion absorbed the 5th and joined East Anglian Reserve Brigade. By November 1917 the battalion was at Crowborough, Sussex and saw out the war in Hastings.

1/6th Battalion (Cyclists)

Attached to 1st Mounted Division, the battalion remained in UK on Home Defence duties along Norfolk Coast. During 1915 the entire establishment of the 1/6th Battalion consisted entirely of 'A1' foreign service men who had volunteered to go abroad as military cyclists, infantry, pioneers or in any other capacity but they were officially informed that the coastal duties entrusted to them were too important for them to be spared – quite a blow to these men filled with patriotic fervour. Towards the end of 1915, however, the 1/6th were relieved of the greater part of their coastal defence duties by a mobile brigade of the Royal Naval Air Service, the battalion retired to become an inland mobile reserve training in drill and trench warfare. In early 1916 the 1/6th Battalion was ordered to furnish a platoon to take over from the London Cyclists at Kessingland, Suffolk. On relief, this platoon (comprising men recruited in Thetford), under the command of young Brandon Officer, 22 year old Lieut. Frank Fison, rode back from Kessingland to North Walsham, a distance of some fifty miles and in a heavy snowstorm, in the teeth of a bitter north-easterly head wind and over roads in shocking condition. The journey was accomplished at a uniform pace of seven mile an hour and with only one casualty. The feat was mentioned in the Regimental History concluding with the comment 'it speaks

A soldier of 1/6th (Cyclist) Battalion, The Norfolk Regiment in 'riding order' at Cromer 1914.

The signallers of 1/6th (Cyclist) Battalion, The Norfolk Regiment, North Norfolk coast 1914.

volumes for the condition and state of efficiency that battalion had attained as military cyclists.' Sadly, the gallant leader of this expedition, Lieut. Frank Fison was later killed in action on the Western Front on 19 July 1916 while serving with The Gloucestershire Regiment.

By 1916 the need for men at the front far outweighed the need for Home Front duties and men of all the cyclist battalions supplied 'an excellent stamp of men for service with the Regular and New Armies in the field' but it would always be a regret expressed by many veterans of the Battalion that they were never allowed to serve abroad together as a unit. By the time of the 'Bug Push' of July 1916 practically the whole of the remainder of the original 1/6th had been drafted to overseas units. For those left in the 1/6th with many new recruits and conscripts they did eventually go overseas – to Ireland, on a stinking cattle boat where every man was sick from the stench alone. While undertaking these peacekeeping duties the battalion was stationed at a number of locations including Tralee, Castle Mayo and Randalstown.

2/6th Battalion (Cyclists)

On 30 September 1914 Lt-Col. Prior wrote to the *Eastern Daily Press* stating the Battalion, although previously having a waiting list for membership, due to 90% of the Battalion signing up for overseas service there was an opportunity for men aged between 17 and 19 years to join both the first and a new reserve battalion. By 20 October 1914 it was proudly announced that the reserve battalion was now full and thus the 2/6th (Cyclist) Battalion was embodied and

Three soldiers from 2/6th (Cyclist) Battalion, The Norfolk Regiment, Bridlington 1915.

a new sobriquet born to a battalion of the regiment the 'Half Crown Holyboys' because of the 2/6 regimental designation and the time honoured nick-name of The Norfolk Regiment and 9th Foot –'The Holy Boys'. After initial training at North Walsham the 2/6th was marched down to Brandon in Suffolk where they expected to be kitted out with full uniform and equipment and their training completed. This was not to be so, in a rapid turn-around the War Office ordered the men of the 2/6th initially to Hornsea and then to Bridlington on the Yorkshire coast.

Telegrams were despatched to the Territorial Association in Norwich and War Office explaining the uniform and equipment crisis and the Commanding Officer was soon authorised to purchase additional clothing. Some four hundred rifles and bayonets arrived first. Uniform did eventually arrive, but only piecemeal – a box of caps, a few tunics, a few trousers and puttees. Kit was a hotch-potch of Victorian Slade Wallace and Valise Pattern equipment, often a belt and only one pouch for ammunition and, if you were lucky enough to be issued a hat, a collar badge or even a shoulder title would have to suffice for the time being in place of a cap badge.

The 2/6th supplied numerous cadres of men and Officers to active service battalions of The Norfolk Regiment and other regiments, but the battalion itself remained in Yorkshire with brief sojourns in Filey and Hunmanby until its' final return to Bridlington where it disbanded in 1918.

3/6th Battalion (Cyclists)

Raised at Norwich in May 1915 this battalion acted as a draft-finding unit with Home Defence Duties. It had one detachment at Worstead commanded by Lt-Col. Dewing where they had a bicycle riding school. This battalion was disbanded in March 1916.

Kitchener's New Armies – The Service Battalions

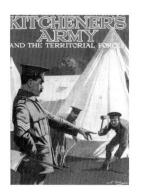

On the 5 August 1914, the day after the Liberal government of Herbert Asquith announced that Britain had declared war on Germany, Field Marshal Horatio Herbert Kitchener,1st Earl of Khartoum and Aspall, was made Secretary of State for War. To many ordinary folk, the choice of a career soldier rather than a politician appeared to be a wise choice for a war minister. Kitchener, or 'K of K' (Kitchener of Khartoum) as he was often known, was a national hero who had come to prominence during the colonial wars of the second half of the 19th century, notably at the Battle of Omdurman in 1898, and later against the Boers in South Africa. The Field Marshal was an illustrator's dream, looking every inch the epitome of the senior British Army officer, and his apparently imperturbable and sternly martial features regularly appeared in newspapers and magazines and on all manner of patriotic souvenirs from Sunday school prize books and certificates to decorative plates and tea caddies. Kitchener was one of few senior British officers far-sighted enough to see that a major European the war was not going to be over by Christmas. To have sufficient numbers of trained soldiers to fight for Britain, a country in which conscription was not introduced until January 1916, he would have to step up recruitment. Kitchener had been opposed the creation of what he termed the 'unwieldy' Territorial Force in 1908 and was not prepared to expand the Territorials to fill the manpower gap. Kitchener wanted a New Army, with soldiers who were proud to say that they were 'Kitchener's men.'

Kitchener Volunteers on the march down London Street, on to Bank Plain, Norwich 1914.

On 11 August 1914 Kitchener's famous call to arms, 'Your King and Country Need You', was published. This called for 100,000 men between the ages of 19 and 30 to enlist; former soldiers were accepted up to the age of 45. The appeal was met with an outburst of patriotic zeal. Recruiting drives were held in every town, and public meetings were led by local dignitaries, with the clergy and military officers delivering speeches voicing 'appeals to patriotism', and military bands filled marketplaces with music as flags and bunting flapped in the breeze. The pressure was on. The British Empire was a force to be

Kitchener Volunteers marching up Guildhall Hill, Norwich 1914.

reckoned with and worth fighting for, while the generation targeted by Kitchener had been educated to possess a sense of duty and obligation to both King and country. The iconic image of Kitchener, with his pointing finger and hypnotic eyes looking directly at a young chap, appeared everywhere. Alongside the Kitchener poster were many others calling for men to 'Join our Happy Throng' and defend Britain and all it stood for from 'the marauding Huns'. Some posters

Volunteers pictured shortly after enlistment at Britannia Barracks 1914.

ignored the appeal to patriotism and instead questioned any man's motives for *not* joining up. One quoted the words of another national hero, the late Lord 'Bobs' Roberts, asking men to 'make sure your reason for not joining is not a feeble excuse', while young women were asked to consider 'Why is *your* boy not in khaki?' Such appeals to patriotism saw groups of young girls arm themselves with white feathers, which could be presented to any coward not thought to be 'doing his bit'.

Both middle-aged and young men adjusted their ages in order to enlist. A tale familiar in most parts of the country tells of young, well-built lads presenting themselves to recruiting sergeants, admitting to be 16 years old (but would pass for 19), and being told to 'go out, then come back in and tell me different'. By 21 August Kitchener had his first 100,000 recruits and what became known as 'K1', the first six divisions of the 'New Army', were approved by the War Office. There were to be five 'New' armies formed under the Kitchener scheme, meaning that most infantry regiments received three New Army battalions.

Rates of pay were clearly laid out in recruitment literature. On enlistment a man would receive seven shillings a week, with leaflets and posters going on to emphasize that food and clothing were provided on top of that. 'Separation

Physical Training for new recruits on Chapel Field Gardens, October 1914.

The future NCOs of the Norfolk Regiment Service Battalions; no uniforms yet but cap badges are worn with pride in the lapel and the all important stripes pinned to their sleeves.

allowances' were also noted: the wife of a soldier with no children received 12s 6d per week separation allowance; a woman with one child got 15s; one with two children 17s 6d; one with three children £1; one with four children 22s; and an additional two shillings per child was paid to families with more than four children. Further financial promises were also made:

> *Provided the Soldier does his share, the Government will assist liberally in keeping up, within the limits of separation allowance for families, any regular contribution made before enlistment by unmarried soldiers or widowers to other dependants such as mothers, fathers, sisters etc.*

The motherless children of a new servicemen each attracted a grant of three shillings a week, exclusive of any allotment (a deduction at source) made to dependants from a soldier's pay. Pay was undoubtedly a deciding factor when it came to recruitment in country areas. August was the traditional harvest month, war or no war, and this was when the best money an agricultural labourer could earn all year (about 21 shillings a week, or three times the basic rate of pay in the Army) was paid. With the Territorials already called up, many farms were short-handed for the harvest. Young men in the towns were under serious pressure to enlist; many country lads held off just long enough to do a few weeks' harvesting and then joined up. This behaviour is clearly reflected in a demographic breakdown of New Army recruitment.

Kitchener men on parade upon the Carrow playing fields 1914.

By September 1914 an average 33,000 recruits were enlisting nationally on a daily basis. Officers were more fortunate when it came to clothing and equipment, although they had to buy their own. There were plenty of local tailors, and national companies such as the Army & Navy Stores that had bolts of serge, barathea and similar cloth of high quality in various shades of khaki and green to supply the needs of newly-enlisted subalterns (Second Lieutenants). For the enlisted men, supplies of uniforms and equipment rapidly ran out, and their resupply was piecemeal. Quartermasters were often seen scratching their heads over the delivery of odd items of uniform. There might be jackets for three men, caps for five, puttees for nine, and assorted items of webbing, such as a crate of 50 ammunition pouches but no belts or cross-straps for them. Clothing factories were running flat out. Most took on more staff and worked shifts right around the clock. A type of webbing equipment made simply in leather with brass fittings was brought in as an emergency measure in 1914, and by 1915 tunics were being run up without fancy details such as pleats in the pockets, but

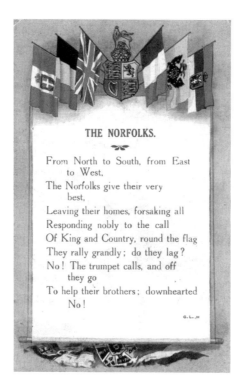

THE NORFOLKS.

From North to South, from East
to West,
The Norfolks give their very
best,
Leaving their homes, forsaking all
Responding nobly to the call
Of King and Country, round the flag
They rally grandly; do they lag?
No! The trumpet calls, and off
they go
To help their brothers; downhearted
No!

G.L.H

still supply could not meet demand. Troops reporting to their allocated barracks and depots were rapidly disillusioned when they were told that there were no uniforms for them. Indeed, there was frequently not enough room to house all the recruits. Some were provided with accommodation under canvas; others were simply handed ground-sheets and a blanket and told to 'make the best of it', sleeping on floors or in countryside close to the barracks until accommodation could be found in barns, maltings or other commandeered buildings. In some areas lucky soldiers were put up by local families at the Army's expense. Other recruits decided to walk home and come back again early in the morning for their first parade. To prevent soldiers returning home at every opportunity, and to begin fostering regimental *esprit de corps*, many of the freshly raised battalions were soon marched off, sent by the train load to training camps in other parts of the country; our Norfolk Regiment Service Battalions were sent to Shorncliffe near Folkstone in Kent. Major H. P. Berney Ficklin of 8th (Service) Battalion, The Norfolk Regiment recalled the early days of the battalion at Shorncliffe: 'The conditions in England at this time were practically indescribable. The men appeared in thousands... all in civilian dress... and had to be found accommodation, food, cooking utensils and boots; and had at the same time to be taught the first principles of soldiering. England owes a very large debt to those ex-non-commission officers who came forward immediately, some of them after ten or fifteen years of civilian life, and placed their experience (rusty perhaps, but albeit of the utmost value) at the service of their country... Some idea of the difficulties experienced in these early days may be gleaned from the fact that there were sixteen men to a tent, and that there was an average of two plates and at the most half a dozen knives and forks to each sixteen men, that tobacco tins had to be used as cups, and that there was a shortage of ablution places and washing materials. The latter were compensated for by taking the whole battalion down to the sea at 5am every morning and making every man bathe.'

A shortage of uniforms could not stop basic military training, which focused on getting men to obey orders without question. Recruits wearing everyday clothes were put through their paces in drill, rifle training and physical exercise, with some demanding compensation for wear and tear, especially to boots. Even knives, forks and spoons had to be shared. A stop-gap measure to compensate for the shortage of uniforms were armbands and regimental cap badges worn on the lapel of the jacket. In some areas unofficial badges were made and worn, but the main drive was to provide some sort of uniform.

In an act of sheer desperation, the War Office introduced 'Kitchener Blues', probably the most disliked uniform in the history of the British Army. The jackets and trousers were sourced from uniform stocks held for postmen, prison

The 'Southrepps Boys' who had joined Kitchener's Army, November 1914.

warders and prisoners, although the uniforms for prisoners tended to be grey and therefore had to be dyed for Army use! This motley collection of uniforms was crowned with a side cap of simple construction.

The Army also looked to its stores and found that its only stockpiles of personal equipment for other ranks consisted of pre-1900 pattern whitened hide pouches, belts and cross straps, worn during the reign of the late Queen Victoria. Unfortunately Kitchener's men did not have the pipeclay to whiten this old equipment, not that there was sufficient go round; most men ended up wearing a belt and one ammunition pouch. Victorian webbing was accompanied by the issue of rifles of similar vintage, and when these ran out, men were issued with wooden 'rifles' and even broomsticks with which to learn arms drill.

The public didn't know what to make of the strange blue uniforms. Some thought that prison warders had been conscripted to maintain public order; others decided that those wearing blue must be Belgian soldiers, and therefore refugees. There were still not enough military buttons and regimental badges to go round, and when khaki uniforms became more plentiful men still ended up wearing collar badges or even buttons in place of a cap badge. To cap it all, much of the cloth had been dyed in great haste, using inferior chemicals. This was partly due to the fact that Britain had relied upon the more advanced German chemical industry for many of its dyestuffs, and what was in stock soon ran out. The inferior dye ran if the uniform became wet or its wearer sweated too freely, turning the skin blue. With typical good humour, Kitchener's men sang a song about their tribulations, featuring Fred Karno, 'King of the Comedians':

Men of a Norfolk Regiment service battalion dressed in their 'Kitchener Blues'.

'We are Fred Karno's Army,
Fred Karno's infantry,
We cannot fight, we cannot shoot,
What blooming use are we?

But when we get to Berlin,
The Kaiser he will say,
Hoch, Hoch, Mein Gott!
What a bloody fine lot,
Fred Karno's sent today!

If der Norfolks
haf gone by, den I kan kom out.

*Lieutenant William
Percival Markwick a
Territorial battalion
Sergeant who took a
commission; he was
killed while serving with
7th (Service) Battalion,
The Norfolk Regiment,
at Vaux Wood during
the Final Advance,
5 September 1918.*

From May 1915 most of the 'Kitchener battalions' were sent to France and Flanders. Training in trench warfare under simulated battle conditions began as soon as they arrived. Each unit spent about a month in training. Everyone became expert in digging trenches and latrine pits. Under the supervision of bawling Sergeant Instructors, the men fixed bayonets and ran to stab and skewer sacks filled with straw hung from gallows, practised firing at targets with the faces of German soldiers printed upon them, and threw both live and practice grenades to prepare them for 'bombing raids' across no man's land. Selected men were trained on machine guns, in sniping, advanced signalling, and firing trench mortars. The Service battalions of The Norfolk Regiment were as follows:

7th (Service) Battalion

K1. Raised in Norwich from August 1914. Raising the Kitchener units was carried out at speed and it was imperative that the volunteers were formed into units as soon as possible and thus the men from Norfolk were despatched to Shorncliffe where the battalion was formally constituted using men from London, Lancashire and elsewhere; only about half the battalion were Norfolk men. Attached to 35th Brigade, 12th Eastern Division the battalion landed at Boulogne 31 May 1915 and joined the front line on 4 July 1915 at Ploegsteert Wood. The first major action for 7 Norfolk came on 13 October from their line in front of the quarries at St Elie. The attack was covered by a barrage but the smoke that was to give them cover stopped before the attack and the men were exposed and many men were instantly cut down by the enfilading enemy machine gun fire. Reinforcements were impossible to send as they were mown down in the first twenty yards. After this action 71 officers and men lay dead, two hundred were wounded and 160 missing.

One story from this failed attack typifies the tragedy of the situation. Twenty-three year old T/Lieut. Thomas Adrian Buckland was one of the 30 Officers who had proceeded to France with the Battalion. In answer to a letter of enquiry from his father into the circumstances of his death he received the following:

> 'In reply to enquiry the OC 7th Norfolk Regt reports as follows: After the attack on 13 October Lieut. Buckland was reported wounded and missing. On the 19 it was reported that 2 men of the 9th Essex Regt [stretcher bearers] went out in front and found Lieut. Buckland who was badly wounded and very weak. One of these men was shot and the other managed to crawl back. It was intended to send another party out on the night of 19-20 Oct. to bring Lieut. Buckland in but the Germans counter attacked that night and after thing were quiet the party went out and found Lt. Buckland dead: apparently he had been shot again.'

In March 1916 the Battalion saw action at Hohenzollern Redoubt. On 1 July the battalion marched to Hennencourt Wood and entered reserve lines behind the embankment of the Albert-Arras railway. During the attack on Ovilliers battalion was in reserve but suffered badly from heavy shelling. In the front line of the Ovilliers sector from 7 August and fought in the attack on Skyline Trench on 12 August where they not only established and held strong points, in each of which one Lewis gun, one machine gun and forty men were left, but also took a number of prisoners. In the attack on Bayonet and Scabbard Trench on 12 October 1916 the battalion ran into heavy enemy machine gun fire from both flanks, the advance continued but before their objective trench was

reached the men of the battalion encountered uncut wire entanglements. After this action just eight officers and 350 men of the battalion left in the trenches.

In April 1917, 7 Norfolk were on the Arras Front in the successful attack on Feuchy Chapel redoubt. On the night of 2-3 May the battalion repulsed a heavy attack upon them in 'Tool', 'Hook' and 'Pick' trenches. Part of Pick Avenue communication trench was penetrated by the enemy and occupied before the men of 7 Norfolk successfully counter attacked. It was soon clear the attack had been far more than a raid, the Germans had intended to occupy the trench, in fact the officers had even set up a mess table including a bottle of champagne – which was consumed with due appreciation by the men of 7 Norfolk. In November 1917 the battalion fought at Cambrai, in this confused and bloody battle over thirty officers and men were killed, almost a hundred wounded and 204 recorded as 'missing.' The final year of the war saw 7 Norfolk deployed on the right of the divisional front on the Lys where they fought the German spring offensive. In August 1918 the battalion was at the front of the autumn offensive starting at Treux on the lower Ancre; attacking, repulsing and counter attacking, in that one month the battalion advanced eleven miles, took 13 enemy machine guns, three trench mortars, one 'granatenwerfer' and sixty prisoners. Over fifty officers and men had been killed and 313 wounded or gassed. In September the battalion was reorganised at Mountauban and fought its last on the Somme at Nurla, taking trenches near Epéhy and finally occupied a sunken road near the Quéant-Drocourt line on 10 October. When the armistice came they were far in the rear of the British front at Landas.

Colour Sergeant Gilliland and Sgt Howard both from 7th (Service) Battalion, The Norfolk Regiment having a shave and a clean up after coming out of trenches, Beaumont Hamel, November 1916.

Hurrah for the
NORFOLKS!

8th (Service) Battalion

K2. Raised at Norwich from September 1914. In its early days it acquired the nick-name of the Businessman's Battalion due to the large number of shopkeepers and workers from the city and county which made up its number. Formally organised and trained, despite initial chronic shortages of uniform and equipment, at Shorncliffe the battalion set off to France from Folkestone on 25 July 1915, part of 53rd Brigade, 18th (Eastern) Division, entering forward lines upon relieving the 8 Suffolk trenches near the Mametz-Carnoy Road. Remaining in the neighbourhood of Albert into 1916 their baptism of fire was to come on 1 July 1916, the First Day of the Somme. The battalion's assembly trenches were just north of Carnoy, their objective, the enemy trenches south-west of Montauban. 8 Norfolk was one of the few battalions to take its objective on the day, but it had cost them 4 Officers and 104 other ranks killed and over two

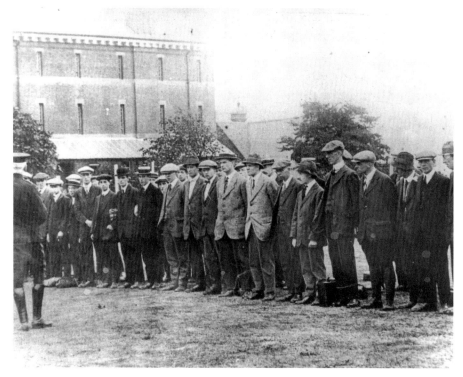

On parade: Men of the Norwich 'Businessmen's Battalion' destined for 8th (Service) Battalion, The Norfolk Regiment.

hundred wounded. On 19 July the battalion was part of a counter attack on Delville Wood. Advancing from the south-western corner of the wood it was hard fighting but the enemy positions were taken, with no little thanks to 2/Lieut Gundry White and his team of bombers. A brave day, but at the cost of almost 300 killed or wounded. Transferring to the Armentièrs sector on 25 September the battalion moved to Wood Post, Authuille Wood in Brigade support for operations at Thiepval. The battle had been costly and the men of 'B' company were left at Crucifix Corner to carry the dead for burial. On 4 October 1916 the battalion was in the successful attack on Schwaben redoubt. On October 21 the Battalion went in again with the attack on Regina Trench and held their gains until relief on 23 October. From 5-8 November 8 Norfolk was at Warloy, here General Maxse, commander of the

18th Division presented decorations and medals for the battalion's actions on the Somme viz; one DSO, six MCs, six DCMs, thirty one MMs and 37 parchment certificates.

The next action for 8 Norfolk was on 17 February 1917 near Boom Ravine, on the left bank of the Ancre, an attack not only made challenging by the enemy shell fire but the slippery sloped terrain also led to sprained ankles and accidents. The battalion was back in the front line on 10 March for the attack on Grenvilliers trench and Irles, a little east of Poelcappelle. In truth, the Germans had been planning to evacuate Irles but the attack chased them out. That achieved, the next objective was to capture Grenvilliers trench and push out certain strong points. It was no mean feat, but the battalion achieved the objective taking many prisoners and sixteen machine guns, with minimal casualties (34 all ranks) for such an action.

The hardest part of the action was mopping up the pockets of Germans who hid down in their 'funk holes' and strong points such as fortified gun emplacements or pill boxes, in one of them alone after this action eighteen Germans held out until a bombing party of two NCOs winkled them out. One of those recognised for his gallantry on this day was Cpl (Acting-Sergeant) Obediah Ellis Smith; the Divisional Commander wrote to him on vellum: "I have read with great pleasure the report of your regimental commander and Brigade Commander regarding your gallant conduct and devotion to duty in the field on 18 March 1917 during the operations against Irles." Smith was awarded the Military Medal for Gallantry in the Field (*London Gazette*: 26 April 1917). This was not to be the last we hear of Smith. The battalion was in action again at Poelcappelle on 22 October. This village had remained a sticking point due to the number of pillboxes the enemy had constructed among the rubble and the terrain all around was deep liquefied mud.

The *Eastern Evening News* of 2 November 1917 published a letter which related an account of the action headed *Victory for the Norfolks*: 'A highly successful minor operation east of Poelcappelle, battalions of the Essex, Norfolk, Suffolk … Regiments captured strongly fortified buildings and concreted redoubts. All our objectives were captured after fierce fighting, and troops pushed on still further … About 200 prisoners captured and heavy casualties inflicted on the enemy … One or two pill box garrisons put up a fight. At one point where a party of Boches looked like putting up a fight of it, a corporal from Norwich [Smith] whose rifle was caked with mud, and whose supply of bombs had run out, actually forced the Boches to surrender by heaving mud at them.' Made up to substantive Sergeant, Smith was later given a commission – no doubt for his powers of quick thinking and initiative.

Poelcappelle was to prove to be the last major action of 8 Norfolk. They held the line at Poelcappelle until they quit the forward trenches in December 1917. In January 1918, 8 Norfolk were in brigade reserve near Elverdinghe and it was here they learned the battalion was to be disbanded. Officers and men were distributed to the Regiments other service battalions, others went to reinforcement camps and entrenching battalions; to quote the Battalion war diary of 20 February 1918, 'The 8th Service Battalion the Norfolk Regiment ceased to exist from today.'

9th (Service) Battalion

K3. Raised at Norwich September 1914, sent to Shoreham and later moved to Blackdown Camp near Aldershot. Reviewed by Lord Kitchener in August, they

RSM Jeremiah Coe, born at West Lexham he was killed in action with 8th (Service) Battalion, The Norfolk Regiment on The First Day of the Somme, 1 July 1916.

Sgt. Obediah Ellis Smith MM, 8th (Service) Battalion, The Norfolk Regiment.

Sgt. Donald Breeze Spalding who lived at 51 Silver Road, Norwich with his wife Leah. Sgt Spalding had served in the South African War and rejoined the colours in 1914 and served in the 8th (Service) Battalion, The Norfolk Regiment. He died from wounds received in action, 2 February 1916 and is buried in Corbie Communal Cemetery, France. He was 36.

Kitchener's Army on the march, Norwich 1914.

proceeded to France on the 30th of that same month as part of 71st Brigade, 24th Division. Formed for the attack on Lonely Tree Hill, west of Hullach on 26 September they were not engaged but received their baptism of fire late on that day when the enemy rained rifle fire on the trenches occupied by 9 Norfolk. Over 200 officers were killed or wounded. Transferred with their Brigade to 6th Division in October the battalion was reinforced and ready for action again. On August 2 1916 the battalion entrained for the Somme front and saw its first major action of the year after taking up lines on the Ginchy-Leuze Wood Road for an attack on The Quadrilateral on 15 September. As 9 Norfolk advanced up the slippery slope the barrage had stopped short leaving a gap of about 200

'At the Front' Lieut-Colonel Bernard Henry Leathes Prior (centre) and the band of the 9th (Service) Battalion, The Norfolk Regiment.

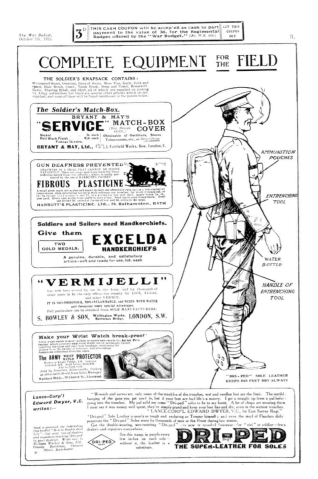

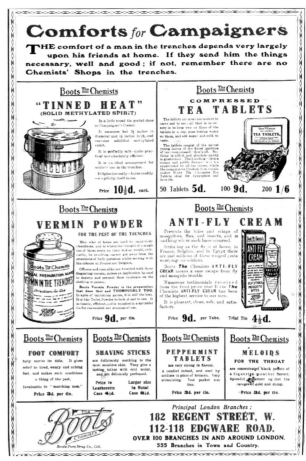

yards in front of the feature, to allow the advance of the tanks and encountered uncut wire that stopped their progress and they were forced to retire to trenches they held until relieved at midnight. The failed attack caused 431 casualties to the battalion.

By the time Lieut-Col Leathes Prior took over command of the battalion (after leaving 6th (Cyclist) Battalion in October 1916 he found it full of fresh drafts with only a small percentage of experienced officers and men left, but he was a great leader and one trusted and respected by his men. On 18 October 9 Norfolk attacked Mild trench. Their attack was delayed by the difficulties experienced by the men mounting greasy parapets and as a consequence much of the protection of the British barrage was lost and the battalion suffered an undue share of German barrage. The men, however, managed to gain positions and consolidated them. Colonel Prior went forward to the position: 'There the garrison holding the trench, despite a good many casualties, were in the best of spirits. They had been heavily shelled, sniped at, and machine gunned, and at least once counter attacked but they had had a success, they had taken the trench, and before I left I felt quite satisfied that they would die to a man rather than lose it.' The first half of 1917 were spent, as the Regimental History describes it 'taking the usual turns of front line, support and reserve, and undergoing the usual enemy shelling in varying degrees.' The battalion was also exposed to gas attacks and men suffered from the constant wet to the degree trench foot became prevalent. They were not involved in major attacks but good officers and men were still being killed and wounded in minor actions, patrols, shell fire and picked off by snipers bullets.

On 20 November the battalion acquitted themselves well at the Battle of Cambrai where the battalion's attack culminated with the capture of Ribécourt.

Captain Gerald Watson Failes DSO MC, 9th (Service) Battalion, The Norfolk Regiment, killed in action on the Ypres salient 15 April 1918. He has no known grave but is named on the Tyne Cot Memorial.

Colonel Prior recorded: 'It would be impossible to set out all the extraordinary incidents of that glorious day: how Hancock and his Sergeant-Major rushed an enemy machine gun position and settled a bet who would kill most Boches. This was won by Hancock, but Sergeant-Major Neale always contends that he was unduly handicapped by having to use his bayonet, whilst Hancock had a revolver. How a runner of 'D' company, without assistance took over seventy men prisoners, including a staff officer. How Worn, wounded in the first hundred yards of the advance, carried on with his platoon until he reached his final objective, the railway station, and consolidated his position... How one man of 'A' company having very daringly and very foolishly penetrated an enemy dug out, leaving his rifle outside, knocked down the Boche who thrust a pistol at his head, seized the pistol and harried his opponent by a vigorous application of the butt end.' The casualties were not as heavy as might be expected for such an action, three officers and 29 other ranks killed, and 62 wounded from all ranks, but we must not cheapen life, these were all somebody's son, brother, father or friend. Colonel Prior wrote of the death of twenty nine year old Major Samuel Blackwell who, after giving a report to the Colonel, and despite being wounded carried on as 'D' Company commander: That was the last I saw of him, for he was killed later on. When the doctor examined his body he found that the first wound was a terrible one; despite which the continued to lead his company, crossed the Hindenburg Line, and initiated the attack against the final objective before being shot dead.'

March 1918 saw 9 Norfolk face the German spring offensive and served in front line trenches on the Ypres salient at Polybecke with headquarters in what was left of Polygon Wood. They marched again in September and joined the allies final offensive at St Omer and fought on by Le Cateau. On 11 November news of the armistice was received by the battalion at Bohain. On 14 November, 9 Norfolk began its march to the Rhine and was the only battalion of the Regiment to enter German territory and form part of the Army of Occupation.

10th (Service) Battalion:
Formed at Walton-on-the-Naze in October 1914 as a Service battalion, part of K4 based at Felixstowe and Colchester. In March 1915 it became a Reserve battalion to find drafts for the 7th, 8th and 9th (Service) Battalions. On 1 September 1916 it became 25th Battalion of 6th Reserve Brigade of Training Reserve.

11th Battalion (T.F)
Raised at Lowestoft in 1915 with Home Service personnel of Territorial Force Battalions. Based at Guildford and Colchester it was disbanded 20 December 1917. (also see 2/4th Battalion)

12th (Norfolk Yeomanry) Battalion
The Norfolk Yeomanry had served in its own right as a unit in Gallipoli and Palestine within the 1st Eastern Mounted division. Men of the Norfolk Yeomanry have the distinction to be the last to leave land during the Gallipoli evacuation. The 12th (Norfolk Yeomanry) Battalion of The Norfolk Regiment was formed from the remaining men of the Yeomanry in Egypt on 11 February 1917. Joining 230th Brigade, 74th Division the battalion served with distinction in the battles of Gaza, Beersheba, Sheria and on the advance of their Division to Jerusalem. Sent to reinforce Western Front, the battalion embarked at

Second Lieutenant Harold Gardiner Cobon MC 'D' Company, 1/1st Norfolk Yeomanry. Born at Paston, a Gresham School Old Boy, he farmed in the village when he left school and had joined the Norfolk Yeomanry pre-war. He had risen through the ranks to Sergeant and took his Commission in April 1916 and won the Military Cross at the Battle of Shiria. He was wounded after the siege of Jerusalem and died of his wounds on 24 January 1918.

Alexandria on 1 May 1918 for Marseilles, landing there on 7 May and joined 94th Brigade, 31st Division and were deployed to Nieppe Forest. On 5 July the battalion CO Colonel Morse was wounded to the degree he did not return to the battalion before the end of the war, he did recover but Yeomanry and Battalion stalwart Captain John Harbord, also wounded at the same time was not to be so fortunate. Twenty-four-year-old John Harbord was the epitome of the patriotic young men of 1914. A native of Norfolk, his lineage could be found in the peerage and the noble old family line of Suffield. Educated at Haileybury School and Clare College, Cambridge, he had been among the officers of the battalion who originally sailed for Gallipoli with the Norfolk Yeomanry in September 1915. He was wounded in the neck by a sniper's bullet on 11 December 1915 and was lucky to escape with his life. After returning to his Battalion he won his Military Cross to North of Jerusalem his citation reads: "For conspicuous gallantry and devotion to duty during an attack. He showed great courage and determination while leading his Company, in difficult country and in the face of heavy fire. He shot three of the enemy and took an Officer and three men prisoners." After receiving his wounds he was removed from the field to Boulogne Military Hospital where he died on 10 July 1918.

The battalion fought through Nieppe Forest and on to Vieux Berquin and further minor operations such as the attack they pressed home, despite considerable opposition at Labis Farm on 19 August, killing many enemy and taking sixty prisoners to boot. Casualties were some of the heaviest experienced by the battalion – eight officers and 38 other ranks killed and over a hundred wounded, such was the cost of 'minor' operations. Divisional Headquarters sent the following to 12 Norfolk: 'Please express to all ranks the divisional commander's appreciation done by the officers, NCOs and men...Plans, however good, do not succeed unless the men display the fine fighting spirit which enabled 12th (Yeomanry) Battalion Norfolk Regiment to overcome strong opposition.' Perhaps, some small comfort for those who had lost old yeoman comrades from back to Gallipoli days in the action.

On 31 October 1918, 12 Norfolk were covering the final advance in the Ploegsteert sector by patrolling the Lys and were involved in one of the last attacks on the north of the Scheldt towards Audenarde. After the end of October the battalion had no more fighting. On 10 November the battalion moved to Avelghem on the Schelt as was there when the Armistice was announced.

1st Garrison Battalion
Formed at Seaford in September 1915 this battalion was stationed in India doing garrison duty in Indian stations from December 1915 until 1920 when the battalion finally returned to England and was disbanded.

Pte Oscar Allcock, son of John and Jessie Allcock, of Tittleshall, Swaffham. Served in The Norfolk Yeomanry and transferred with the battalion to 12th (Norfolk Yeomanry) Battalion, The Norfolk Regiment. He died of wounds on 2 October 1918, little more than a month before the end of the war.

6 The Auxiliary War Hospitals

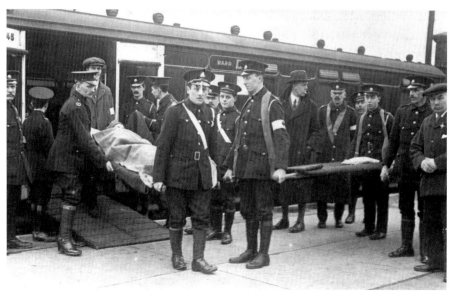

Lady Leicester, leading light in the creation of The British Red Cross Society in Norfolk.

High up in the Tribune Gallery of Norwich Cathedral is a banner emblazoned with full colour depictions of the entwined badges, armorial bearings and mottos of The British Red Cross Society and The Order of St John of Jerusalem. Trimmed with distinctive black and white tassels the banner is no ordinary standard or colour as it measures some eight feet by six feet. It is not mentioned in any guidebook nor does it have an explanatory note displayed beside it. Only by making a special request and undertaking the awkward journey up a small winding stone staircase in the turret by the Great West Door and then observing the reverse of the banner is there any clue obtained to its purpose and significance. Beneath a fine layer of dust the gold leaf lettering which covers it spells out the legend;

> 'To the Glory of God. This banner was presented by The British Red Cross Society and the Order of St John of Jerusalem in the County of Norfolk... To Commemorate for Ever the Work of Tending the Sick and Wounded in the following Hospitals during The Great War 1914-1919.'

Beneath the legend is a list of 62 Norfolk towns and villages and locations in the City of Norwich, all of them Auxiliary War Hospitals. These were not large and specifically constructed buildings erected across the county but rather village halls, public buildings and above all large private residences turned over by their owners for the treatment and convalescence of returned wounded servicemen during The First World War.

Headquarters staff of the Norfolk Branch of the British Red Cross Society c1915.

The Walsingham Red Cross VAD Detachment 1914.

The story of the auxiliary war hospitals began a year after the creation of the Territorial Force when, the War Office issued its *Scheme for the Organisation of Voluntary Aid in England and Wales* in 1909. The War Office had recognised that in the event of a major European war, which seemed ever more likely, that existing medical arrangements for its armed forces would be wholly inadequate. Some form of supplementary aid would be required, in addition to the Territorial Force Medical Service, to provide transport and care for the thousands of casualties returned from a British Expeditionary Force on the continent.

The British Red Cross Society and Order of St John, (although at that time working as separate Voluntary Aid Societies) immediately began to establish so-called Voluntary Aid Detachments (VADs) to recruit and train local volunteers for the task.

There were no mixed detachments. Male detachments were the most difficult to recruit as they required 56 volunteers, headed by a Commandant, with a Medical Officer, Quartermaster and Honorary Secretary, Pharmacist and four sections, each comprising a Section Leader and 12 men.

'Pat' one of hundreds of young ladies from the county who volunteered to do their bit in the Auxiliary War Hosptals.

The emergency hospital set up in the Swaffham Assembly Rooms for the annual inspection of the local detachment, July 1914.

A women's detachment of 24 was far easier to raise. Led by a Commandant and Lady Superintendent (a trained nurse) the detachment comprised four sections, each with a Section Leader and four women, or two sections each with one Section Leader and nine women. Within its ranks, each the female detachment had to include four proficient cooks.

To become full and proficient members of their Voluntary Aid Detachment, girls were expected to train for and pass examinations in both first aid and nursing. The male detachments trained in first aid only, and in war they served mostly in corps responsible for the transport of the wounded, setting up and furnishing the Auxiliary War Hospitals and acting as ward orderlies; but the VAD (a term applied to all serving in the VAD system, but more especially to the nurses) were to 'regard himself or herself as part of the Medical Organisation of the Territorial Force, available to serve in the event of war.'

In Norfolk a total of 64 male and female Voluntary Aid Detachments (VADs) had been registered in locations all over the county between October 1910 and July 1914; personnel had been trained, and many had staged exercises, setting up emergency hospitals in public halls, schools, tents and even cricket pavilions. Some of the last exercises in the county were recorded in a feature which appeared in the June 1914 edition of *The Red Cross*. The types of exercise carried out were quite specific and adopted very similar themes; they are, in retrospect, chillingly accurate predictions of the shape of things to come;

'The Annual Inspection of Detachments 12 and 25 was held in Swaffham recently. A practice was first held to which visitors interested in the proceedings were admitted. In accordance with the scheme drawn up by the Commandant of No.12, Mrs Critchley Martin, the Assembly Rooms were formed into a temporary hospital, with kitchen adjoining. The large ballroom was used as a casualty clearing station by the Men's Detachment under Commandant Mr F W Cooper. The supper room was furnished as a ward of eight "beds" and at the end of the long room the Quartermaster, Mrs Murray Gaurie, had the hospital equipment. The Men's Detachment has only been raised a year, and it was the first time the two detachments had worked together in front of the public. The arrangement was most successful. The inspection was made by Major Knox MD, RAMC who expressed himself most satisfied with what he had seen.'

A similar report was given for Walsingham Detachment, who fitted up a temporary hospital in the Oddfellows' Hall in the village. The main hall being divided into two wards, medical and surgical; eight 'patients' were treated. Later that same month during the Territorial Army encampment in the grounds of Holkham Hall a combined display of ambulance work was made by the Territorials and VADs from Walsingham and Wells. Arrangements were made for the disposal of 50 'wounded' at Wells where the VADs had made a Hospital in the Church Hall. All arrangements for nursing the said 'cases' were carried out to the satisfaction of Major Freeman RAMC, who was inspecting the Territorials. Two months later the Voluntary Aid Societies were mobilized for war.

On the outbreak of war, public meetings were held in Norwich and in towns and villages to ascertain which public buildings and houses were available for conversion to Auxiliary War Hospitals. Many families offered a spare bedroom, and municipal buildings such as schools and concert halls were made available. However, the need to concentrate convalescent servicemen in one place made their dispersal in ones and twos a nonsense, while many municipal buildings were required for their original purpose, even in time of war. In most cases a large local house or the rectory proved to be the most practical place in which to open a hospital, although hospital 'annexes' were opened in public buildings

*Members of the No 15
Detachment, City of
Norwich British Red
Cross and members of
the RAMC removing a
soldier from the first full
ambulance train of
wounded brought to the
county at Thorpe
Station, Norwich
29 September 1914.*

or other houses when returning casualties overwhelmed the bed space available. Nationally, to avoid duplication of effort the Red Cross and St John also agreed to join forces for the duration of the war.

In the early days of war urgent appeals headed 'On behalf of The Red Cross' had appeared in local newspapers and features were run on the preparations for 'Red Cross Hospitals' (as they became known across the country during the war) at South Walsham, Cromer, Norwich, East Dereham and Great Yarmouth and many more were announced over the following days.

By 8 August a Comforts Depot was established in The Lazar House, Norwich. Here members of the public could take supplies for and make donations to the Red Cross Hospitals. Local businesses such as Garlands and Chamberlins rapidly began stocking medical uniforms and hospital supplies and took out large adverts in the local press to advertise what they had in stock. By 13 August the recruitment drive for volunteer nurses was announced by the headline 'To the Women of Norwich.' On Thursday 20 August the *Eastern Daily Press* announced, with great pride, 'The First Auxiliary Hospital in Norfolk has opened its doors at Lakenham Schools.' The newspaper's claim was somewhat inaccurate; although set up by the Red Cross the Lakenham Hospital was always intended to be a military reception hospital that would act as an overspill for The Norfolk and Norwich Hospital. The first true Auxiliary Hospital to receive wounded was at Woodbastwick; it was here that the first convalescent wounded were brought after their arrival on an ambulance train at Thorpe Station, Norwich on 29 September 1914.

The readiness of the VADs is well evinced by the fact that another 26 fully staffed and equipped Auxiliary War Hospitals from across the county had opened their doors to convalescent troops by the end of 1914. The numbers of wounded coming to Norfolk were increasing to such an extent that the Norfolk and Norwich Hospital had to erect prefabricated buildings to create new wards. The County Asylum at Thorpe had its patients removed and was turned over to become The Norfolk War Hospital in April 1915. The Wayland Infirmary near Attleborough was also taken over as a military hospital in April 1917. Both the major Norwich hospitals needed to expand yet further and put up marquee tents in their grounds to create yet more wards. The Auxiliary War Hospitals played an essential role in the treatment and convalescence of wounded and sick servicemen. It should also be noted that although there were fluctuations, the numbers treated in the Norfolk Auxiliary Hospitals steadily rose throughout the war.

Wartime recruitment of VADs was never a problem, as most were inspired by patriotism and a sense of doing their bit, while soon the 'Romance of the

Left: Removing one of the first returned wounded brought to the county from Thorpe Station direct to Woodbastwick Hall Auxiliary War Hospital.

Right: The prefabricated building wards erected outside the Norfolk and Norwich Hospital for returned wounded soldiers c1915.

Red Cross' became a term which featured heavily in newspapers, books and magazines.

Girls wishing to nurse had to be 'presentable,' and must provide a reference or recommendation from a local doctor, priest or magistrate. They also had to be able to give time to their duties on a regular basis. In 1915, with the introduction of the 'General Service' section of the VAD, there were a wide variety of duties for girls of most abilities, so most could find a place: as a cook or laundress, a clerk, typist, telephonist, driver, chauffeur – or VAD nurse.

Convalescent troops, doctors and nursing staff at the Norfolk and Norwich Hospital c1916.

The premier position of VAD nurse was often the preserve of the young ladies from local middle-class families who could afford to give the time, pay for the lectures and had £1 19s 2½d to buy a uniform (although later in the war local VAD units did have funds to issue uniforms, or at least replace worn out aprons, collars and cuffs). Officially, VAD nursing members had to be 23 to 38 years old to serve in military hospitals but if girls looked old enough and were keen enough they would get in. Girls as young as 17 became VADs, especially in the more rural Auxiliary War Hospitals. They were appointed on two weeks' probation. If found to be suitable, they would be *expected* to serve for up to three months, and many served for much longer. The engagement of VAD members could be terminated if 'at any time they were found unfit in any respect for service'.

Most of the hospitals in Norfolk had a 'family' atmosphere, with the owner of the house or his wife as commandant of the detachment, and VADs drawn from its domestic staff and local girls. The care supplied was directed by a

Left: A typical scene of ambulance column traffic outside Thorpe Station c1915. Often young ladies would gather at the entrance and throw flowers into the back of the passing ambulances.

Right: The Norfolk War Hospital (the emptied Thorpe Asylum) 1915.

*The first batch of
wounded brought to the
Norfolk War Hospital.*

Medical Officer (often a local doctor) and the Superintendent (a trained nurse).
In the early years of the war many of these professionals provided their services
free of charge, and some did so throughout the war, but payments were allowed,
with a Medical Officer drawing £1 a day. Matrons, Sisters-in-Charge and Ward
Sisters paid one guinea (£1 1s) a week, and staff nurses (with two years' training)
£40 a year. The VAD nurses who served part-time in their local hospital were
unpaid, but expenses for board and lodging, laundry (up to a limit of 2s 6d)
and travel to and from the hospital could be claimed,. There was also a
Compassionate Fund which assisted sick or injured VAD personnel.

The term 'nurse' for the VADs was one which some members of the public
objected to as VADS were 'not fully trained' so the Joint War Committee took
pains to publish the following clarification and endorsement of the VADs:

*Tent wards erected in the
grounds of the Norfolk
War Hospital 1915.*

*There is not, and never has been, any reasonable doubt as to what
constitutes a fully trained nurse… In every large hospital there is a
matron, and there are sisters, staff nurses and probationers. The Matron
and sisters are addressed by their titles, but Staff Nurses and Probationers
are alike addressed as 'Nurse'. A probationer of only one day's standing
would consequently be called, for example, 'Nurse Jones'… It was,
therefore in accordance with the usual practice that a VAD member
engaged in the nursing department of any hospital should be called
'Nurse'.*

Role and rank were defined by the colour of indoor uniforms. Commandants wore a conspicuous bright scarlet dress, Quartermasters grey, Cooks pale brown and the Nurses, the iconic pale blue dress. All were expected to have the correct clean white headgear, and starched detachable collars and cuffs. The Nurses' aprons were not issued with a red cross on the breast, so they had make their own, and because there were no guidelines for the dimensions of the cross, you will rarely see any two in photographs that are quite alike. To appear more experienced, young nurses quickly put their aprons through the wash a few times so that the red cross grew lighter, while some VADs were not above using a bleach to 'pink' their cross. Legs were clad in black stockings, with skirts at ankle-length, worn with the boots or shoes currently in vogue.

Some of the returned wounded convalescing in Norwich c1917.

Outdoor dress for nurses consisted of a long, single-breasted greatcoat and a distinctive cloth hat with a metal Red Cross badge. A Commandant wore a smart two-piece jacket and skirt, blouse with collar and tie, their insignia of rank displayed on the cuffs, topped by a fine black or dark navy straw or felt hat with a ribbon and badge. The nurses preferred to parade in their distinctive dresses, so photographs in outdoor dress are rare. In the early years of the war VADs were encouraged to wear Red Cross 'brassards' (armbands) and to carry

*Woodbastwick Hall
Auxiliary War Hospital
1915.*

*'Keeping the boys
amused' at
Woodbastwick, May
1915.*

*Mrs C. Gaze, Matron of
the Diss Auxiliary War
Hospital.*

their 'identity and authority to wear' card to identify them as Red Cross workers. In theory, this gave them the protection of the Red Cross in the event of an invasion. The card and armband were also to be carried while wearing civilian clothes in the event of emergency (especially air raids), to show that they had been trained in first aid.

To provide 24-hour cover, VADs worked shifts, girls arriving on foot, riding bicycles or being dropped off by pony and cart. Although they may have been assigned certain core duties, no two days would be quite the same for a VAD. Convalescent men were allocated to the hospitals from two sources. Some would be dispatched on trains or by ambulance after treatment in the main county or district War Hospital. Some would come almost direct from France having passed through continental field hospitals with 'Blighty wounds' which, if they only required basic treatment and convalescence, could mean that men were sent directly to an Auxiliary War Hospital, many still in their muddy and bloody uniforms.

A telegram would be sent to the hospital commandant to alert her of the arrival of fresh wounded, and if they were not delivered by ambulance, a reception committee would have to be dispatched to the local railway station. In many rural areas there were no ambulances, and hastily converted delivery

vehicles and private cars were used, along with a motley collection of wheel-chairs and hand-drawn carriages, with VAD escorts for the walking wounded.

At the hospital, the VADs and male orderlies would assist the storekeeper in exchanging khaki for the flannel 'hospital blue' uniform of jacket and trousers, white shirt and red tie worn with the soldier's own cap and boots for trips out of doors (slippers being issued for inside wear). The soft and shapeless 'blues' aided the identification of any wandering serviceman who'd slipped out, perhaps for a strictly against the rules pint! Times of blues shortage, or particularly heavy numbers of returning wounded, can be noted in old photographs, with convalescent troops still wearing their khaki uniforms.

Left: Colne House, Auxiliary War Hospital, Cromer 1915.

Right: 'Dunrobin' the Annexe to the Red House Auxiliary War Hospital, Cromer c1915.

Eva C. Cheetham OBE, Matron of the Cawston Manor Auxiliary War Hospital.

Cawston Manor Auxiliary War Hospital 1915.

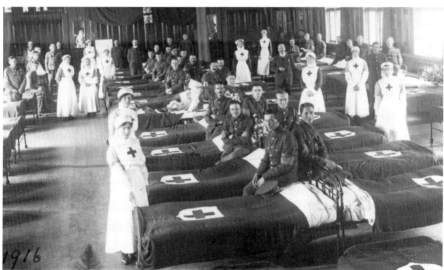

Foresters Hall, the overflow for the Auxiliary War Hospital at The Towers, Downham Market c1916.

East Dereham War Hospital 1915. Based in the Vicarage the owner Rev. Macaughton Jones was Commandant, his wife Quartermaster. The remarkable number of 2067 convalescent troops passed through this hospital between the years 1914-1919.

Mrs W. H. Macaughton Jones, Quartermaster of the East Dereham Auxiliary War Hospital 1915.

Mrs Agnes R. Palin ARRC, Commandant of the Fakenham Auxiliary War Hospital.

Are we Downhearted ?
NO not at FAKENHAM !

A typical day began with nurses assisting those patients marked 'Up' to rise, shave, wash and dress before breakfast. Some patients would be marked 'Up from and to', the specific times of day set by the Medical Officer (MO). Patients ordered 'bed rest' would be made to look presentable for the MO's inspection rounds. The nurses would follow the MO, Commandant and Lady Superintendent during this inspection. Those patients able to stand to attention would snap to it by their beds, the conscious bed-bound lying at attention. Once the MO's rounds were over, the VAD nurses would assist the MO and Lady Superintendent in changing dressings. Young VADs were daily confronted with sights that would haunt their dreams for the rest of their lives. One former nurse who had served at the Attleborough Auxiliary War Hospital recorded the story of a young soldier whose head was completely swathed in a heavy bandage; something she had never seen before. As she slowly unwound the bandage she wondered if there could actually be a head left inside its folds.

Throughout the day, bedpans and sputum cups had to be supplied and emptied, and Nelson's inhalers used to clear congestion on the lungs. The incapable would be fed, and those learning to walk again helped on to crutches or supported. To occupy convalescent troops most wards had been gifted a host of comforts, such as gramophones, books and magazines. Crafts such as rag rug making and embroidery were taught to the bed-bound. Many VADs patiently helped the wounded to write home, took dictation or read letters to the blinded, always doing their best to remain cheerful. There were regular teas and concerts held at the hospitals to help keep up morale or help to raise funds. The VADs would help the convalescent troops to make decorations, such as paper link chains and Chinese lanterns. If there was a sports element – such as cricket – involved in such an event, the convalescent soldier might bat while a local Boy Scout, recruited by the nurses, would be the soldier's runner.

Many VADs kept autograph books in which their patients were encouraged not just to write a message or rhyme but to draw a picture of, say, his cap badge, to

FIRST-AID INSTRUCTION CLASSES

Weekly Classes of Instruction in all branches of First-Aid and Ambulance Work will be given in the Corn Hall, commencing MONDAY, AUGUST 20th. next, at 8 p.m.

A special appeal for Recruits is made to men under and over military age, and to those who are ineligible for ordinary military service.

Former Members of the Men's Detachment whether Volunteers or otherwise are cordially invited to attend to assist and also to keep in touch with Ambulance Work, this invitation specially applies to the Police who are so frequently called upon to render first aid.

The importance of a knowledge of First-Aid is obvious.

No fees are charged.

F. W. COOPER, Commandant.
W. B. RIX, Secretary.

Men's Detachment, Norfolk, 25
British Red Cross Society.

Harleston Auxiliary War Hospital.

Nurses assisting on the stalls at the fete to raise money for the Soldier's Comfort Fund and their Auxiliary War Hospital in Harleston.

Staff and convalescent troops at Hedenham Hall Auxiliary War Hospital c1916.

Hoveton Hall Auxiliary War Hospital 1915.

Prince Edward Home Auxiliary War Hospital, Hunstanton 1916.

Staff and convalescent troops at Prince Edward Home Auxiliary War Hospital, Hunstanton, May 1917.

paint or draw his vision of home, happy memories, flowers, birds or cartoons. A few of these books have survived as deeply moving records of the thought and feelings of the thousands of servicemen from all over the world who were treated in the Norfolk Auxiliary War Hospitals.

By 1916 many of the hospitals in Norfolk were equipped with all the basic necessities but many were able to boast advanced equipment such as minor surgery theatres, "apparatus for massage and electrical treatment" and x-ray

machines. The most outstanding evidence for the standards and efficiency of the Auxiliary Hospitals in Norfolk are the recovery statistics. It is estimated that the number of deaths of troops in Norfolk Auxiliary hospitals was about one in every three hundred and the average stay of patients in the hospitals to recovery and discharge was almost a whole day below the national average.

By 1918 Norfolk had provided over sixty fully equipped Auxiliary Hospitals for convalescent troops through the duration of the war but the achievements of the British Red Cross Society and Order of St John working groups, which backed up or were allied to the Auxiliary Hospitals are no less significant. The Lazar House Auxiliary Hospital Supply Depot handled 102,339 items throughout the duration of the war. The Rest Room or 'Soldiers and Sailors Rest Home' in the yard of Thorpe station was described in the *British Red Cross Society Norfolk Branch Report* of 1918 as 'consistently full' and the demands on the volunteers who staffed it were 'heavy and continuous.' The report went on to state;

> 'It is night work and of necessity does not come much into public notice but the fact that 23,000 men have been given shelter, rest and food during the two years it has been open testifies that these volunteers have been undergoing fatigue and self-sacrifice of an arduous character.'

Yet, even more remarkable was the service provided by the BRCS Norwich Transport Company. Their job was to collect the wounded and convalescent soldiers from Thorpe Station, Norwich and to run them to The Norfolk &

Left: *Cliff House Auxiliary War Hospital, Hunstanton 1915.*

Right: *The staff of Cliff House Auxiliary War Hospital, Hunstanton 1915.*

Staff and convalescent troops at Loddon Auxiliary War Hospital, June 1918.

Left: *Mrs Sarah Gamzu Gurney MBE, Commandant of the Ingham Auxiliary War Hospital.*

Right: *The Day Room at Ingham War Hospital.*

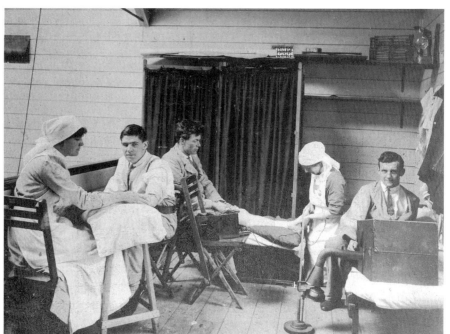

Treatment Room, Ingham.

Lower House Auxiliary War Hospital, Mundesley Road, North Walsham 1915. Mrs Edith Wilkinson Carter was Commandant, Major Long RAMC the Medical Officer, Nurses Murrel and Wilkinson were the leading nursing staff and Boy Scout W. Foulser was the runner.

Left: *Edith Wilkinson-Carter ARRC Commandant of Lower House Auxiliary War Hospital, North Walsham.*

Right: *Convalescent troops and staff at 'Wellingtonia' Auxiliary War Hospital, Mundesley Road, North Walsham 1915.*

Convalescent troops and staff at Swainsthorpe Auxiliary War Hospital 1915.

Norwich, Lakenham Military or Norfolk War Hospitals for assessment and treatment (if necessary) before despatch to an Auxiliary Hospital. The 1918 *Annual Report* outlined their achievements;

> During the past year the services of the Norwich Transport Company have again been utilized to the fullest extent. The number of convoys received was 87 comprising 10,041 patients, the majority of whom were stretcher cases, bringing the total since the beginning of the war up to 317 convoys and 40,498 patients, The numbers are slightly less than last year, as in the early part of the year there was a comparatively quiet time, but after the German offensive started in March until the end of October there was no cessation of work, added to which the cases were particularly severe for the most part, which made the past nine months the most arduous and exacting period the Transport Company have faced. The geographical position of Norwich made it necessary for the city to invariably have the last train despatched from Dover sent here, with a result that for weeks a convoy never arrived before 2am.

The report goes on to point out that about 30 men have served in the Company for the entire duration of the war, 'among them Quartermaster Mann who has attended every convoy except one.' It points out

M. Grace Holloway Commandant of 'Wellingtonia' Auxiliary War Hospital, Mundesley Road, North Walsham.

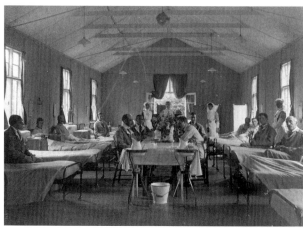

Left: *The Diss Auxiliary War Hospital, Uplands House, Walcott Road 1915.*

Right: *The Long Ward at the Town Close Auxiliary War Hospital, Norwich 1915.*

Mrs Alice Jarrold, Commandant of 'Sunny Hill' Auxiliary War Hospital, Thorpe.

Walsingham Auxiliary War Hospital.

it was from this same company that two men were drawn to serve in the Rest Centre every night and helped to man the 24 hour air raid shelter on the station. The report concludes; 'Of the rank and file upon whom this work devolved I cannot speak too highly. Discipline, cheerfulness and enthusiasm, even during the most trying times have never been lacking.'

Norfolk did perform well; out of the 61 counties with Auxiliary Hospitals in them Norfolk was one of only 19 with more than 1,000 beds available between 1915 and 1918. Out of those 19 Norfolk was one of the 15 who were able to run their hospitals and a cost of less than 4s. per patient, per day. Norfolk was below the national average time for the amount of time patients occupied their beds or convalesced and was below the national average for deaths in convalescence. It is also notable that with net receipts from donations to the Norfolk VAS of almost £15,000 a year since 1914 provided a third of the total running costs of the Auxiliary War Hospitals in Norfolk were met by public donations and subscriptions.

Between 1918 and early 1919 the last of the convalescent soldiers were discharged from the Auxiliary Hospitals across Norfolk and the Hospitals were gradually closed, decommissioned and 'returned' to the private use of their owners. The 62 Auxiliary Hospitals in the county had provided some 1377 beds, through which passed 27,446 convalescent soldiers who had been cared for by a total of 35,736 VAD Nurses, orderlies, drivers and volunteers drawn from both VAS in the county. The last BRCS and OStJ Auxiliary Hospital run under the VAD system in the county at Reedham, East Dereham, Downham Market and Ditchingham closed in April 1919. The last of the convalescent soldiers aided by VAD Nurses were at the Wayland Military Hospital, which finally closed on 26 April 1919.

On Saturday 18 October 1919 a service of Thanksgiving was held at Norwich Cathedral, conducted by the Dean and The Bishop of Thetford. Towards the end of the service, and before a packed congregation, the Dean and Chapter accepted the Banner marking the work of the British Red Cross Society & Order of St John Auxiliary Hospitals in

*Commandant Mrs
Maude Cator and the
staff of the
Woodbastwick Hall
Auxiliary War Hospital.*

*Convalescent troops on
the river at
Woodbastwick.*

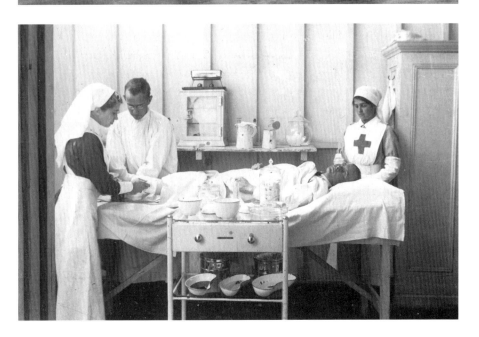

*The operating theatre set
up at Woodbastwick
Auxiliary War Hospital.*

Left: *The staff of Wroxham Auxiliary War Hospital 1914-17.*

Right: *The Wymondham Auxiliary War Hospital at 'Abbotsford' on Vicar Street 1915.*

Norfolk during the First World War for "permanent preservation in the Cathedral." The Countess of Leicester, then President of the Norfolk Branch of the BRCS, made the presentation. Following the Cathedral Service a 'Meeting of Tribute' was held in the Agricultural Hall, which, like the service, attracted a vast crowd. At this meeting Sir Arthur Stanley (The man who would prove to be chairman of The Joint War Committee through both World Wars) gave

Staff, orderlies, nurses and convalescent troops at the Great Yarmouth Auxiliary War Hospital.

The ambulance of the Great Yarmouth (1st Norfolk) Voluntary Aid Detachment bringing wounded to the Auxiliary War Hospital.

The hardworking men of The Norwich British Red Cross Society Transport Company, during the war they transported over 40,000 wounded.

Staff of 'The Dales' Auxiliary War Hospital for Officers, the Royal Marine was the hospital batman.

Members of Norfolk British Red Cross Society 'Reserve' in France.

After the war the Norfolk War Hospital returned to being the Norfolk County Mental Hospital. On 29 November 1921, in a special ceremony, many of those who had worked there returned to see Earl Haig unveil a plaque to commemorate the hospital's role throughout the Great War.

Presentation of the Banner marking the work of the British Red Cross Society & Order of St John Auxiliary Hospitals in Norfolk during the First World War for 'permanent preservation in the Cathedral' at a Thanksgiving Service Saturday 18 October 1919.

an address and brought with him a message from Lt. General Sir Charles Burtchaell, KCB who had been Director General of the Army Medical Services in France;

'It is impossible for me to speak too highly of the way the nursing of our sick and wounded was carried out in the private and other Hospitals of the British Red Cross Society and Order of St John during the war. I had complete confidence that any patients admitted to these hospitals would not only have the very best standards of treatment but would be skilfully and sympathetically cared for … the nursing staff were beyond praise.'

The Auxiliary War Hospitals of The British Red Cross Society & Order of St John

Norfolk
1914-1919

PLACE	OPERATIONAL DATES	PATIENTS ADMITTED
Attleborough *Town Hall*	26 November 1914 – 22 November 1917	656
Brancaster	11 December 1914 – 14 February 1915	31
Brundall	12 October 1914 – 1 October 1916	712
Buckenham Tofts	1 January 1916 – 25 May 1916	52
Catton	2 September 1915- 4 February 1919	687
Cawston	12 November 1914 – 21 February 1918	2,884
Cromer *Red House* *Colne House*	1 October 1914 -10 December 1917 11 March 1915 – 31 January 1919	734 634
Diss	9 September 1914 – 24 January 1919	1,651
Ditchingham	1 November 1914 – 26 April 1919	240
Downham Market	19 February 1915 – 14 April 1919	1,274
East Dereham	16 November 1914 – 5 April 1919	2,067
Fakenham	1 June 1915 – 21 January 1919	480
Felthorpe	11 November 1914 – 14 January 1919	432
Garboldisham	7 November 1914 – 19 January 1919	324
Hardingham	1 May 1917 – 20 November 1917	305
Harleston	5 May 1917 – 7 April 1918	136
Hedenham	3 April 1915 – 23 December 1918	771
Hingham	2 October 1915 – 23 December 1918	200
Holkham	1915/16	30
Hunstanton *Cliff House* *Prince Edward Home* *Convalescent Home*	5 February 1915 – 31 January 1919 1 July 1916 – 31 January 1919 19 June 1915 – 28 February 1916	440 869 190
Ingham	29 October 1914 – 28 January 1919	1,082
Kirstead	7 November 1914 – 30 December 1918	391
Letheringsett	9 December 1915 – 25 January 1919	1,082
Loddon	19 November 1914 – 23 November 1918	474

PLACE	OPERATIONAL DATES	PATIENTS ADMITTED
Lynford Hall	22 June 1918 – 28 January 1919	49
Matlaske	16 October 1914 – 7 October 1915	144
Melton Constable	18 December 1915 – 31 January 1919	399
North Walsham		
Lower House	11 November 1914 – 20 March 1919	714
Wellingtonia	25 January 1915 – 31 January 1919	475
Norwich		
Bracondale	25 November 1915 – 28 March 1919	956
Town Close	26 November 1914 – 1 August 1915	600
Town Close Lodge	10 August 1915 – 19 February 1919	2,087
The Convent of the Little Sisters of the Assumption	9 November 1914 – 17 December 1918	361
The Palace	23 April 1918 – 4 March 1919	276
Overstrand	3 November 1914 – 6 April 1916	65
Reepham	26 November 1914 – 5 April 1919	1,158
Saxlingham	8 July 1915 – 28 September 1915	22
Sheringham		
Knowelside	29 October 1914 – 31 January 1919	957
The Dales	1 July 1918 – 10 January 1919	71
Swainsthorpe	2 October 1915 – 3 February 1919	663
Thetford	19 January 1915 – 28 April 1915	102
Thorpe St Andrew		
Coonor	30 November 1914 – 9 December 1918	608
Sunny Hill	2 January 1915 – 30 November 1918	1,152
Thornham	5 January 1915 – 31 January 1919	617
Walsingham		
Berry Hall	20 October 1914 – 7 September 1915	110
Oddfellows Hall and Lower Farm	22 February 1915 – 31 December 1918	384
Weasenham	19 October 1914 – 19 October 1915	102
West Bilney Manor and Narborough Hall	26 March 1915 – 8 June 1918	607
West Harling	7 November 1914 – 31 December 1918	130
Woodbastwick	28 September 1914 – 1918	1,113
Hoveton & Wroxham		
St Gregory's	6 May 1915 – 22 January 1919	810
Hoveton Hall	29 October 1914 – 13 August 1917	284
Wymondham	26 November 1914 – 31 January 1919	803
Yarmouth	29 November 1914 – 17 January 1919	815

7 Keep the Home Fires Burning

'Doing their bit' – Women and the War

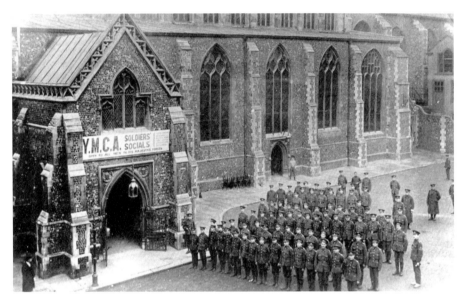

St Andrew's Hall, Norwich c1915 – the biggest YMCA centre in the county.

The County of Norfolk answered the 'Call' magnificently when war came. Local lads joined the armed forces by the thousand and the city, towns and villages from whence they came supported them throughout the war by holding an amazing array of events, socials and drives with such novel titles as 'Flag and Fag Week' to raise money, make and donate items to send 'comforts' to the boys 'at the front,' the wounded and prisoners of war. Most towns and villages had an Auxiliary War Hospital nearby and there was never a shortage of young ladies

The YMCA soldier's 'hut' in the Church Rooms, North Walsham c1915.

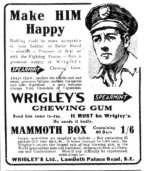

who wanted become VADs (both 'Immobile' for local duties and 'Mobile' for duties anywhere in the country or abroad). There were also YMCA 'huts;' if in a town they tended to be in converted buildings and church rooms like the one in North Walsham or, if near a village or on an army camp in an actual wooden barrack hut that were usually given names such as 'Aline Hut' on Bulmer Road in Winterton. In Norwich the main YMCA centre for troops was in St Andrew's Hall, used by thousands of soldiers every week. By 1918 the Association county headquarters in St Giles controlled twenty five YMCA 'huts' across the county, many of them with the troops along the North Norfolk coast; all of them providing soldiers with food, drink and free writing paper and envelopes and requiring friendly Christian ladies and gentlemen run them.

The staff of the Norwich General Post Office c1915.

The Swaffham Assembly Rooms, used as a soldier's canteen c1915.

A 'young kiltie' from The Black Watch, stationed at Taverham Hall 1916. Special orders were given to these troops regarding the use of the stairs on trams when wearing a kilt. Naughty tricks were known to be played by the rowdy girls from the Vinegar Works a favourite was to drop a hanky, let the 'scottie' pick it up, but as he did so a female accomplice would come up from behind and throw his kilt up.

Many ladies had taken over simple clerking and shop work in local businesses that had a 'vacancy' left by a man gone to war – but that said, most employers took on female staff on the strict understanding that it was only a stop gap measure and that when the man returned he would be able to have his job back; and most ladies were quite happy with the arrangement – it was the patriotic thing to do.

However, there was a potential army of women who wanted to do *something* for the war effort but were simply not being utilised. The Women's Suffrage Movement had suspended its militant action to allow a concentration on the war effort so when they felt they were not being used effectively the country could expect the women would soon find a way of voicing their desire. It took a combination of events in 1915 to really get women mobilized into munitions work.

The sea change began with what became known as the 'Shells Scandal' of 1915, after the publication of the startling revelation that in the opinion of Sir John French the British Commander-in-Chief, a shortage of munitions led directly to the failure of the British offensive at Neuve Chapelle in March 1915. The Liberal Chancellor, David Lloyd George fervently believed radical improvements were required in the munitions industry if we were going to carry on what was now appearing to be a prolonged war against Germany. The 'Shells Scandal' became a key factor in the fall of the Liberal Government in May 1915 and the establishment of a new coalition in which the new Ministry of Munitions was created under Lloyd George.

On 21 July 1915 numerous ladies from the county had travelled down to the capital for the 'Women's Great Procession' where some 30,000 women marched through the capital under the banner of 'We Demand the Right to Serve.' The pressure was on and as a direct result of the scandal munitions work was expanded and after the march women were going to do their bit too!

At this juncture I feel it is worthwhile pointing out that in the First World War the term 'munitions' did not just refer to the manufacture of shells but a whole host of operations from pulling flax crops (used for industrial purposes and in textile manufacture) to manufacturing wooden boxes for military purposes and even working in the various stages of aircraft manufacture – broadly speaking, if it involved 'feeding the guns' of the war effort it could be titled munitions work – so a girl could have been involved in munitions throughout the war and never touched a gun shell!

*Violet Jackson the
Trunch postwoman,
'for the duration'.*

The times were changing and the labour exchanges across the county displayed the poster 'War Service for Women' calling for women to enter their names 'at once' on the Special Register of Women for War Service indicating that in particular women were required locally for 'farm work, dairy work, leather stitching, brush making, clothing machining and light machining for armament' with the advice 'But even if you have no special experience in any of this work, you should register. It may be possible to train you. It is certain that as more men join the forces, more women will be wanted to work while they are away. Even if you can work only half of each day, you may be useful.'

Even more women were taken onto the workforce in 1916 as the introduction of conscription saw thousands more men leave their places of work to serve in the forces. Ladies were working in jobs which female labour would have been taboo in the years before the war. Across Norfolk women were employed in such diverse occupations as 'clippies' on buses and trams, working on the railways, as post women and working the 'rounds' driving horses and carts for local businesses as diverse as the butcher, the dairy and the general dealer. Extant factories were often given new, but allied items to produce for the war effort, many expanded their premises and their workforce was supplemented by women at various levels along the production line; Hobbies of Dereham produced munitions, Savage of Lynn, previously an agricultural and fairground machinery maker went into aircraft wing manufacture, Mann Egerton made a number of different aircraft including short bomber and seaplanes. Boulton & Paul Ltd also went into aircraft production and made 2,530 aircraft (notably FE. 2bs, Sopwith Camels and Snipes) and 7,835 propellers in their Norwich factories. Also in the city, Barnards Ltd Engineers produced over 6,994 miles of wire netting to the War Office and Admiralty and hundreds of prefabricated wooden barrack buildings. The ready-made clothing department of Chamberlins was dedicated to the manufacture of khaki clothing supplying the War Office, Norfolk territorial units and volunteer battalions as well as serving contracts for oilskins, the GPO and Government munitions factories and F. W. Harmer literally supplied two tons of clothing a day to assist the war effort from its St Andrew's Street factory. Caleys made thousands of bars of their famous marching chocolate and Jarrold's printed the letter headed paper for YMCA, Church Army and Navy and Army Canteen Board as well as

*Women workers at
Arthur Preston's gravel
pits – 'no job for a lady
in peacetime.'*

Some of the girls from Boulton & Paul's aircraft manufacturing factory, note the letters B.P. printed on their overalls.

making thousands of pocket wallets and stationery designed for Christmas gifts to the fighting men at the front. Above all, at this time Norwich was a city of shoe manufacture. Howlett & White Ltd, just one of a number of large scale boots and shoe making businesses in Norwich made 453,000 pairs of boots and shoes for the British Army, 32,000 for the Allies and 21,000 British Aviation Boots. Some factories entirely passed over to war work and proudly displayed the sign 'His Majesty's Factory' above the door.

Several local lasses went off to serve in the National Explosives Factories. National Filling Factories and major factories employed in the manufacture of explosives and gun shells around the country. A few Norfolk factories were adapted for various single stages of shell production such as Norwich Components Ltd who made fuses, Laurence & Scott who made shells for 60-pounder guns and Burrell's of Thetford where they produced shells in their the machine shop and turnery at St Nicholas Works, while the boiler shop made Admiralty gun mountings. The girls working in munitions tended to have been predominantly from domestic service backgrounds with a liberal smattering of shop assistants, laundry workers and clerks and similar working/lower middle class occupations. Requirements were similar to any other occupation in this

Left: Norwich munitions workers in the 'National Shell' overalls c1916

Right: A fine line up of Norwich 'Munitionettes' 1916.

The munitions girls from Laurence & Scott's in Norwich c1916.

employment sector, basic education and physical fitness to do the job was enough. The days were long, many factories working flat out 24 hours a day with girls working 12 hour shifts, typically 6am to 6pm and vice versa for the next shift. Although there were great disputes over the inequality of wages – men were paid an average of £4 6s. 6d. whereas women only received £2 2s. 4d but most girls were quite happy because the wages were higher than they were accustomed to before the war and are recorded as saying 'I thought I was very well off earning over two pounds a week.'

The girls working with explosives would be expected to come to work in 'working clothes' but would be typically issued a pair of wooden soled clogs (sparks caused by metal cleats or 'blakies', studded or even plain leather soled boots are not a good idea when working with explosives). In the most critical areas the girls wore fabric slippers or even rubber gumboots. All munitions workers working on the likes of armaments or aircraft were issued the relevant pattern of 'National Shell Overall' which comprised a draw string or elasticated cap and a flame retardant canvas or cotton twill overall with a belted waist. Soon numbered brooch and button fitted badges were issued to the workers with entitlement card which had to be carried at all times along with their general issue identity cards to show the worker was entitled to be in the factory, although it must be noted that these badges or indeed any metal item be it the likes of a brooch or even a clothes fastening such as a steel button were prohibited in the danger areas.

The dangers many of these girls were exposed to were very real, stringent precautions against sparks or employees having a crafty smoke were founded on practical knowledge and awareness of tragedies in the industry when minor explosions had been caused, killing a number of workers. Another danger was from over exposure to the chemicals in cordite and especially TNT which could turn hair a gingery colour and skin yellow, hence the girls became nick-named 'canaries'. Despite warnings from doctors girls kept on working and after a few serious illnesses and fatalities it became common policy to send batches of the 'canaries' off to coastal resorts to clear their systems.

Because of the nature of work and requirement of mobility the shell overall outfit was soon supplemented with trousers – something no young lady would have been seen wearing on the street before the war. This additional item of clothing was worn as a badge of honour on the street by the munitions girls, who soon acquired the nick-name of 'munitionettes.' Although the eyebrows of many of those who still held Victorian values many have been raised, they could hardly complain because these girls were 'doing their bit' and any criticism could be seen as unpatriotic. It is certain that many of the munitions girls took brave steps forward in public behaviour and through the war years began wearing trousers, having short hair cuts (the girls were told to keep their hair short as long hair, even if braided, could get caught in the factory machinery and metal hair grips, combs etc were all considered contraband), going to cinemas unaccompanied by a man, smoking cigarettes and drinking in public houses. The girls soon got into their stride organizing entertainments, pantomimes, theatrical productions and even (shock-horror to the blue stockings) playing organized games of football! The girls were also known for getting up to mischief – woe betide any kilted Scottish soldier passing the gates of the Norwich vinegar works at knocking off time!

Norfolk Forage Company, Army Service Corps (formerly Women's Forage Corps), Cantley Chaffing Store Staff 1917.

In the early years of the war Queen Alexandra's Imperial Military Nursing Service (QAIMNS), First Aid Nursing Yeomanry, Women's Forage Corps (1915) and The Women's Legion (1916) were the main women's units serving with or with close attachment to the military or War Office. The year 1917 heralded the creation of two more uniformed military services for women. Many local girls saw their chance to get out of the county, seek adventure and do their bit in uniform by volunteering for service in the new women's forces of the Women's Auxiliary Army Corps (later re-titled Queen Mary's Auxiliary Army Corps), Women's Royal Naval Service (WRNS; popularly and officially known as the 'Wrens') both formed in 1917 and the Women's Auxiliary Air Force formed in 1918 for the express purpose of substituting women for men in non-combatant roles. Earlier in the war such units would have been looked at askance but such had been the revolution in the role of women in the war great pride was shown in the girls joining up. They often went in small groups like those from Edwards & Holmes Ltd boot and shoe factory (early in the war they had made thousands

Wren Officer, Womens Auxiliary Army Corps and war workers at Pulham airship station 1917. Each woman holds an item representing the type of work she was doing.

of uppers for Cossack boots for the Russians) on Drayton Road who proudly sent their girls off under the banner of 'They are doing their bit.'

On the Land

The County War Agricultural Committee had existed since the outbreak of war when all County Councils had been requested by the President of the Board of Agriculture and Fisheries to set them up to ascertain the needs of farmers and the best means of assisting them in cultivating their land, training women for farm work and to develop the agricultural resources within each county. Further District sub-committees were established across the county. Their duties included the survey of uncultivated land, the registration of all holdings over 5 acres, co-ordination of supply and distribution of manure, and of cultivation of crops and vegetables and allocating temporary labour. Sub committees also monitored what happened to the land in their area and questions would be formally put to land owners who reduced their productive land – even the clergy did not escape as one Norfolk vicar received a roasting for erecting a tennis court on land that could have been used for growing food. Even the army got involved when in March 1918 the Army Council urged that 'every opportunity should be taken to cultivate lands in and adjacent to barracks.' To encourage this the Commander-in-Chief in each command was to appoint a Command Agricultural Committee of Officers – I bet they were delighted.

By 1917 the cold wet winters began take their toll on the country. In Norfolk the Brandon River had burst its banks and caused serious flooding at Southery

Men from 3rd (Special Reserve) Battalion are proud to be photographed with their fine crop of cabbages, grown under the War Office scheme to cultivate land around barracks and permanent army camps.

Fen and Hockwold in 1915; the spring of 1916 was wet and snowy affecting spring sowing and hours of sunshine through the year were markedly reduced, hardly the best recipe for a good harvest to support a country in wartime. The year 1917 did not start much better, the cold winter having dragged with frost experienced in Norwich up to the 18 April. The channel was far from clear in February 1917, the German Navy sank 230 ships bringing food and other supplies to Britain. The following month a record 507,001 tons of shipping was lost as a result of the U-boat campaign. Britain feared a war of attrition and in direct response to this the Board of Agriculture set up the Food Production Department (FPD) to organise and distribute agricultural inputs, such as labour, feed, fertiliser and machinery, and increase output of crops. The FPD officials had a wide range of emergency powers to enforce proper cultivation to the degree they could cross private property, dispossess inefficient tenant farmers and order new land to be ploughed up and new, streamlined, seven man Agricultural Food Executive Committees were established that drove on the land work and reinforced the policies of the FPD.

The floods at Southery 1915.

Although women had worked on farms in dairies, butter making, poultry keeping and at harvest time for generations before the war, more joined them as the men went away to war. There were a few voluntary organisations in operation such as The Women's Farm and Garden Union and the Women's National Land Service Corps (later known simply as Women's Land Corps), and The Land Service Corps that had made one of its most important objects the organization of village women into working gangs under leaders, but it was not until 1917 that the Women's Land Army was formed. Initially there was scepticism about the ability of women 'taking the place of a man' on a farm

A fine study of a Women's Land Army worker in Norfolk 1917.

Mrs Burton Fanning presenting arm bands to Land Army Girls at Mr J. Thistleton-Smith's farm, West Barsham, 1917.

A Norfolk land girl feeding cattle 1917.

from the farmers, and from the public generally. Then there was the question of billeting, a consideration of 'the loneliness of farm work' and wages. To address these matters and recruit the girls the Board had in place Women's Agriculture Committees in each county, headed in Norfolk by Sir Ailwyn and Lady Fellowes. County Offices were opened and Organising Secretaries appointed, in Norfolk it was the energetic Miss Burgess but in such a large agricultural county her work would have been a lot harder without the keen assistance from Honorary Secretaries Mrs Parish and Miss Burton. Then followed the appointment of the Travelling Inspector for Norfolk and Suffolk, Mrs Harvey who supervised the work in areas, and of Group Leaders in the villages. Recruitment campaigns were voiced through the press and at open air rallies. On 24 July 1917 the Norfolk Women's War Agricultural Committee met at the Shirehall. In her opening remarks The Hon. Lady Fellowes pointed out, with some pride and aware of the drive behind them, that all the WWAC Committees in the county now belonged to the Board of Agriculture Food Production Department. Lady Fellowes reported that 'according to actual returns they had over 5000 women now working on the land in Norfolk' she also announced: 'Under the National Service Scheme, centre for training girls for work on the land had been opened as follows: Mr W. Case, Gateley, with accommodation for 15 girls; Mr G. Overman, Weasenham, 4; Mr W R Harvey, Illington, 6; Miss Godfrey, New Buckenham, 1; Mrs Oswald Ames, Thornham and Mrs Betts, Thornham each with accommodation for 2. These girls were trained for four weeks, after which situations were found for them for various work on the land'... They were provided with an outfit, and their railway fares were also paid. Though it did include breeches she thought there was nothing in the outfit to which the most particular person could take exception.'

The complete uniform issued to the girl consisted of a knee length tunic with a button fastening integral belt, boots and gaiters or puttees, soft hat and breeches which were cut to measure for each girl. After three months' proficient service each girl would receive her official armlet – a loden green band with a bright red crown upon it. Despite initial scepticism the efficient organisation and training of the Land Army girls proved their worth to the farmers. The key to the situation was that the weather also improved, food production was up and the wheat harvest of 1917 was the best in our history.

Despite this great achievement there was still a fear among many people that the country was running out of food. Panic buying and hoarding food had manifested to varying degrees since war was declared. A Ministry of Food was established in December 1916 but throughout 1917 the Government had been concerned about the nation's food stocks and the particular shortages in sugar, flour and potatoes but had been reluctant to impose rationing, it was suggested instead that people may wish to adopt 'The National Scale of Voluntary Rations' of 4lbs of bread or 3lbs of flour, 2½lbs of meat and ¾lb of sugar per week. This became a matter of patriotic pride and many families signed pledges and placed red, white and blue pledge cards headed 'In Honour Bound' in their windows to show their support. To help the situation the County War Agricultural Committee organised food economy lectures across the region particularly extolling the virtues of pickling vegetables and bottling fruit, special economy recipes appeared in the newspapers and books like *Our War-Time Kitchen Garden* by Tom Jerrold (1917) informed us about not only what we can grow in our garden but also our dietary needs emphasising that we can still remain 'the bull-dog breed without the roast beef of old England.'

Alice Allison of Trunch in her Women's Land Army uniform 1918.

Rationing

The Ministry of Food requested local authorities to appoint Food Control Committees in August 1917. Their membership was to be 'composed of persons well acquainted with local conditions and possessing the confidence of the public'. The Ministry's intention was to limit membership to twelve, of which at least one had to be a woman and one a representative of labour. In fact, the stipulated membership was generally exceeded and included farmers as well as local food retailers. On 17 December the Food Control Committee (Local Distribution) Order 1917 was made giving the local Food Control Committees powers to introduce measures for local food control. This entitled the committee to a wide discretion over the type of rationing scheme to be adopted and the foods to be controlled (subject to approval from Food Controller, Ministry of Food) and even vary the maximum prices of milk, bread, flour, butter, cheese, fish, potatoes and rabbits and requisition supplies of milk or buy and sell it.

Unfortunately voluntary rationing and Food Control Committees were not enough, the myth of 'there's only three week's food supply in the whole country' persisted and people were still hoarding as in the fear there was going to be an imminent food shortage so the Ministry of Food was left with no other option and made the decision to introduce mandatory rationing in January 1918 with the primary intention of being able to guarantee supplies, not to reduce consumption. Sugar was the first to be rationed, later followed by butchers' meat for the whole country in February and for the very first time the people of Britain were introduced to ration books. Rationing now covered sugar, fats (ie butter, margarine and lard) butcher's meat and bacon. Any

NORFOLK CONSTABULARY
NOTICE!
SHOOTING HOMING PIGEONS
Killing, Wounding or Molesting Carrier or Homing Pigeons
is punishable under the Defence of the Realm Regulations by
SIX MONTHS' IMPRISONMENT OR £100 FINE.
The public are reminded that Carrier and Homing Pigeons are doing valuable work for the Government, and are requested to assist in the suppression of the shooting of these birds.

A REWARD of £5
will be paid by the General Officer Commanding Northern Army, Home Defence, for information securing conviction for killing or concealing Naval or Military Carrier Pigeons.
Information should be given to the Police or nearest Military Post or to the General Officer Commanding Northern Army, H. D., Norwich.

Any person who finds a Carrier or Homing Pigeon dead or incapable of flight and who neglects forthwith to hand it over or send it to some military post or police constable in the neighbourhood with information as to the place where the pigeon was found; or, having obtained information as to any Carrier or Homing Pigeon being killed or found incapable for flight, neglects forthwith to communicate the information to a military post or to a police constable in the neighbourhood is liable, on conviction, to the punishment above described.

J. H. MANDER, *Captain,*
County Police Station,   Chief Constable.
Castle Meadow, Norwich,
November 1917.
Roberts & Co., Printers, Ten Bell Lane, Norwich.

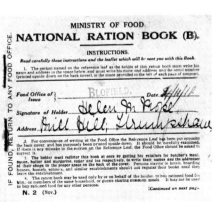

MINISTRY OF FOOD.
NATIONAL RATION BOOK (B).
INSTRUCTIONS.
Read carefully these instructions and the leaflet which will be sent you with this Book.
1. The person named on the reference leaf as the holder of this ration book must write his name and address in the space below, and must write his name and address and the serial number (printed upside down on the back cover), in the space provided to the left of each page of coupons.

person found deceitfully using their ration book faced a stiff penalty of a fine of up to £100 or six month imprisonment – or both.

Numerous cases were brought before the magistrates; George W. Wilkin, confectioner, bread and biscuit baker of Jetty Street, Cromer is a typical example. The Cromer Food Control Committee had found evidence of Mr Wilkin obtaining a larger amount of sugar than he was authorised to receive. He argued that he had been supplying large quantities of cakes and buns to the local troops and he had not broken any rules because the extra sugar he had was in fact his brother's unwanted quota. His brother was Albert Wilkin, a grocer from Aldborough. Albert was brought up at the same time and accused of making false statements on his sugar returns to the Erpingham Rural District Food Control Committee. The Bench convicted both, fining George £10 and £4. 17s costs and Albert £1 and £5 7s costs – in the days when these fines were imposed £5 equated to a lot of Norfolk men's monthly wage. Similar cases were also brought before the Norwich City magistrates as well as cases of food adulteration, especially adding water to milk, sawdust to flour and a host of bulking up products to butter. Most tried pleads of ignorance adding they just wanted the goods to go farther in these times of need. They were fined, a hundred years earlier they would have ended up in the city pillory.

Local Heroes

Just a cursory glance through the pages of any local newspaper during the First World War finds Norfolk men in all the major battles and theatres of the widening war (as well as many women working 'at the Front'.) Often dramatic, gallant and tragic incidents and actions are mentioned in letters home from the men who were there; moving and remarkable these are the first hand testimony of heroes. There also proud tales of boys from across the county winning decorations on land, sea and air all over the world. But one legacy still remains above all, that of The Victoria Cross, our nation's highest military decoration awarded for 'most conspicuous bravery, or some daring or pre-eminent act of valour or self-sacrifice, or extreme devotion to duty in the presence of the enemy.' Since its' inception by Queen Victoria in 1854, to date, just over 1,350 have been awarded, these are the stories of our Norfolk Regiment and County VCs awarded during the First World War.

CSM Harry Daniels VC, MC

The county of Norfolk's first recipient of the VC during the First World War was CSM Harry Daniels, 2nd Battalion, The Rifle Brigade. In every way he is the *Boy's Own* story book hero. He was born on Market Street, Wymondham, on 13 December 1884, the thirteenth child of a local baker, tragically both his parents died while he was still a young boy. Put in the Norwich Boy's Home on St Faith's Lane had had a number of adventures running away and living in the countryside, on one occasion he had even been out on a fishing trawler. He tried to join the army under age on several occasions until he just passed for old enough to be a boy soldier and enlisted into The Rifle Brigade. Always a fit, keen and daring man he shone at sports and gymnastics and spent time on a tour of duty in India before the war. He steadily rose up the ranks, by 12 March 1915 Harry was a Company Sergeant Major in the third day of the ill-fated offensive at the Battle of Neuve Chappelle, France. 'A' and 'B' Companies had been virtually annihilated. Just before 5.00pm 'C' and 'D' received the order 'Attack in fifteen minutes' He could see his company faced a mass of wire en-

CSM Harry Daniels VC, MC.

tanglements that remained uncut just 15 yards from the trench, the men would get caught on this and with intense machine gun fire from the enemy it was nothing sort of suicide. Calling to his pal Cpl Cecil Reginald 'Tom' Noble to 'Get some nippers' they both went over the top into a hail of bullets. They were both wounded almost immediately but they kept cutting until their job was done when 'Tom' took a fatal bullet in the chest. Harry, although badly wounded, managed to crawl back. For their gallant actions they were both awarded the

One of many depictions of CSM Harry Daniels winning his VC.

Victoria Cross. Harry returned to Norwich to a hero's welcome, the streets were lined with cheering well-wishers and he was presented with the Freedom of the City, but did not forget to go and visit his old boy's home. 'Dan VC' was commissioned a few weeks later and he went on to be decorated again with the Military Cross for another action. After a distinguished military career, and an appearance on the British team at the 1920 Olympics, he retired as a Lieut-Colonel in 1942 and joined 'civvy street' as a manager at the Leeds Opera House. He died at Leeds on 13 December 1953, his last request being that his ashes should be scattered on Aldershot cricket pitch.

CSM Harry Daniels gives a wave from his carriage window as he departs after his hero's return to Norwich.

Sergeant Harry Cator VC, MM, CdeG

Sergeant Cator was Norfolk's most decorated soldier. Born on 24 January 1884 the son of a railway worker at Drayton and was educated at Drayton School. He married on 2 September 1914 and enlisted the following day. He proceeded to France with 7th Battalion, East Surrey Regiment on 23 June 1915. He was given his first award, The Military Medal for Gallantry in the Field in 1916 during the Battle of the Somme for helping to rescue thirty-six men who had become tangled in enemy barbed wire in no-man's-land he was also decorated with the Croix de Guerre avec Palme (France).

Harry's VC was awarded for action at Hangest Trench during the Battle of Arras. His citation states the award was: 'For most conspicuous bravery and devotion to duty. Whilst consolidating the first line captured system his platoon

Sergeant Harry Cator VC, MM, CdeG.

Cpl. Sidney James Day VC.

suffered severe casualties from hostile machine-gun and rifle fire. In full view of the enemy and under heavy fire Sergeant Cator, with one man, advanced to cross the open to attack the hostile machine gun. The man accompanying him was killed after going a short distance, but Sergeant Cator continued on and picking up a Lewis gun and some drums on his way succeeded in reaching the northern end of the hostile trench. Meanwhile, one of our bombing parties was seen to be held up by a machine gun. Sergeant Cator took up a position from which he sighted this gun and killed the entire team and the officer whose papers he brought in. He continued to hold that end of the trench with the Lewis gun and with such effect that the bombing squad was enabled to work along, the result being that one hundred prisoners and five machine guns were captured.' Three days later he was severely wounded by a bursting shell which shattered his jaw. He recovered from his wounds and was presented with his VC personally by HM King George V at Buckingham Palace 21 July 1917.

After the war Harry worked for a time as a postman in Norwich and then with the Unemployment Assistance Board. During the Second World War he joined up again and became a Captain Quartermaster with 6th Battalion Norfolk Home Guard and later the Commandant of a prisoner-of-war camp in Cranwich. He passed away at the Norfolk and Norwich Hospital at the age of 72 on 7 April 1966 and is buried in Sprowston Cemetery, near Norwich.

Pte. Sidney James Day VC

Sidney Day was born in Norwich on 3 July 1891 at 4 St Ann's Lane, St Julian, Norwich, this was one of the 'hard up streets' of Norwich, many good honest hard working folk lived here – these tenements were all many could afford. The property was demolished in the city slum clearances of the 1930s. Sidney's father, William was a storekeeper for a local brewery and money was tight with a number of other children's mouths to feed. There were four sisters called Ethel, Rosa, Edith, Alice and one brother, Harry. Three other siblings died when they were very young. Sidney was educated at St Mark's School, Lakenham and worked as butcher when he left school. Day was seriously wounded in four places during the Battle of the Somme and was invalided back to England where he spent several months in hospital near his home in Norwich. When he was discharged, he returned to France as a Corporal serving with 11th Battalion, The Suffolk Regiment. He won his VC while in the line at Priel Wood, Malakoff Farm, east of Hargicourt, France on 26 August 1917. His citation published in the *London Gazette* 17 October 1917 reads:

> 'No. 15092 Cpl. Sidney James Day, Suffolk Regiment (Norwich). For most conspicuous bravery. Cpl. Day was in command of a bombing section detailed to clear a maze of trenches still held by the enemy. This he did, killing two machine gunners and taking four prisoners. On reaching a point where the trench had been levelled he went alone and bombed his way through to the left in order to gain touch with the neighbouring troops. Immediately on his return to his section a stick-bomb fell into the trench occupied by two officers (one badly wounded) and three other ranks. Cpl. Day seized the bomb and threw it over the trench, where it immediately exploded. This prompt action saved the lives of those in the trench. He afterwards completed the clearing of the trench and established himself in an advanced position, remaining for sixty-six hours at his post, which came under intense hostile shell,

grenade, and rifle fire. Throughout the whole operations his conduct was an inspiration to all.'

Day also returned to a hero's welcome in Norwich but on his return to France was wounded and taken prisoner. After the war and back on 'civvy street' Sidney Day did a variety of jobs, in the 1930s he ran his own tea rooms at Landport in East Sussex. The building was destroyed by bombing in 1941. Day then became a messenger in Portsmouth Dockyard but had to retire in 1948 after developing TB. Sidney Day died on 17 July 1959 and is buried in Milton Cemetery, Portsmouth.

Lieutenant-Colonel John Sherwood-Kelly VC, CMG, DSO

The Norfolk Regiment obtained its only Victoria Cross in The Great War at the Battle of Cambrai when John Sherwood-Kelly (37) an Acting Lieutenant-Colonel of the Norfolk Regiment, was on detachment Commanding 1st Battalion, Royal Inniskilling Fusiliers. On 20 November 1917 at Marcoing, when a party of men were held upon the near side of a canal by heavy rifle fire, Lieutenant Colonel Sherwood-Kelly at once ordered covering fire, personally led his leading company across the canal and then reconnoitred, under heavy fire, the high ground held by the enemy. He took a Lewis gun team, forced his way through obstacles and covered the advance of his battalion, enabling them to capture the position. Later he led a charge against some pits from which heavy fire was coming, capturing five machine-guns and 46 prisoners.

Lieutenant-Colonel John Sherwood-Kelly VC, CMG, DSO.

Lieutenant Gordon Muriel Flowerdew VC

Gordon Flowerdew was born to Arthur and Hannah Flowerdew at Billingford Hall, near Scole in the Waveney valley, on 2 January 1885. After attending Framlingham College, at the age of seventeen, he emigrated to Canada and worked as a cowboy and later took up farming. He joined Lord Strathcona's Horse, a cavalry regiment, on the outbreak of the war and rapidly gained his commission and was soon serving in France with the Canadian Expeditionary Force.

On 30 March 1918, an attack was planned for French troops to take the town of Moreuil to the south of a wood, while three mounted squadrons of the Royal Canadian Dragoons to led the initial attack, which was then to be followed up by men from Lord Strathcona's Horse, their object to take an adjacent wood. The Canadian Brigade was to attack in three separate but converging thrusts. Two squadrons of Lord Strathcona's Horse were to attack the wood on foot, with 'C' Squadron, commanded by Lieutenant Flowerdew to make a mounted attack, one of the last of its kind to be staged on the Western Front. The attacking force encountered strong resistance and there was a great deal of hand-to-hand fighting, but by late morning the northern section of the wood had been captured by the Canadians. It was at this moment that Lieutenant Flowerdew, his sword raised, led his men to almost certain death in a suicidal attack on two lines of the enemy, each with about sixty men and three machine-guns.

The *London Gazette* of 24 April 1918 published the citation that reveals what happed next: 'For most conspicuous bravery and dash (NE of Bois de Moreuil, France) when in command of a squadron detailed for special service of a very important nature. On reaching the first objective, Lieutenant Flower-dew saw two lines of the enemy, each about sixty strong, with machine guns in

Lieutenent Gordon Muriel Flowerdew VC.

the centre and flanks, one line being about two hundred yards behind the other. Realising the critical nature of the operation and how much depended upon it, Lieutenant Flowerdew ordered a troop under Lieutenant Harvey, to dismount and carry out a special movement while he led the remaining three troops to the charge. The squadron (less one troop) passed over both lines, killing many of the enemy with the sword, and wheeling about galloped at them again.

Although the squadron had then lost about 70 per cent of its numbers, killed and wounded, from rifle and machine gun fire directed on it from the front and both flanks, the enemy broke and retired. The survivors of the squadron then established themselves in a position where they were joined, after much hand-to-hand fighting, by Lieutenant Harvey's party. Lieutenant Flowerdew was dangerously wounded through both thighs during the operation but continued to cheer on his men. There can be no doubt that this officer's great valour was the prime factor in the capture of the position.'

He is buried in Namps-au-Val British Cemetery, Department of the Somme, France. Flowerdew's gallantry was immortalised further by Sir Alfred Munnings in his painting the 'Charge of the Canadian Horsemen.'

Corporal Arthur Henry Cross VC MM

Born on 13 December 1884 at Shipdham, one of five children. When he was fifteen he moved to London, married at 17 and was a father by 19. He enlisted in the 21st Battalion (First Surrey Rifles), The London Regiment on 30 May 1916 and transferred to the Machine Gun Corps in 1917.

Promoted to Lance Corporal in the 40th Battalion, Machine Gun Corps, on 25 March 1918 at Ervillers, France he volunteered to make a reconnaissance of the position of two machine-guns which had been captured by the enemy. With the agreement of his sergeant he crept back alone with only a service revolver to what had been his section's trench that was now occupied by the enemy. He surprised seven soldiers who responded by throwing down their rifles. He then marched them carrying the machine guns complete with the tripods and ammunition to the British lines. He then handed over the prisoners and collected teams for his guns which he brought into action immediately, annihilating a very heavy attack by the enemy.

The following June he was awarded the Military Medal for another act of bravery. He later returned to visit Shipdham and was presented with an engraved watch and more recently a road was named in his honour in the village. For the making of the film 'Carrington VC' (1955) starring David Niven the producers felt it would be more realistic if Niven were wearing a real VC, and put out an appeal in newspapers, this was answered by Cross who brought his medal personally to the location.

Arthur Cross died on 26 November 1965, in Lambeth, London and was buried at Streatham Vale Cemetery, London in a simple ceremony (at his own request), beside his second wife, Minnie and their children Terrence and Mary, who were killed during the London blitz in 1941.

Edith Cavell – A heroine in a league of her own.

Norfolk's and our Nation's greatest heroine of the war was, Edith Louisa Cavell. Born at Swardeston on 4 December 1865 the daughter of the Revd. Frederick and Mrs. Louisa Cavell; her father was vicar of the village for a total of 45 years. As she grew up Edith showed a natural love of nature and always surrounded herself with plants and animals. Some of her sketches, paintings and

Cpl Arthur Henry Cross VC MM.

drawings of birds she saw and plants she collected from the common are still known and treasured in the village today.

While at school Edith showed a flair for French, after working in a few positions as a Governess she took a post with the family of prominent Brussels advocate M. François in 1890. A firm favourite with the family, she was with them until 1895 when Edith returned to Swardeston to nurse her father through a brief illness. Having helped restore her father to health Edith made her life affirming decision to take up nursing as a career. Edith applied and was accepted to become Assistant Nurse, Class II at the Fountains Fever Hospital in Lower Tooting. To obtain her general hospital training, Edith applied to and was accepted at the London Hospital as a probationer in April 1896. The following year a typhoid epidemic broke out in Maidstone and Edith was one of six London Hospital nurses seconded to help; out of the 1,847 people who contracted the disease, only 132 died. Edith received the Maidstone Typhoid Medal for her work here; it was the only medal she was ever to receive from her country. Edith spent a number of years in private nursing but found her strongest calling was to those in dire need, such as those suffering from disease or among

Edith Cavell: Christian, Patriot and Martyr.

the sick poor in London and Manchester. In 1907 she returned to Brussels and was soon appointed Matron heading the École Belge d' Infirmières Diplômées, often simply referred to as the Clinique, it was a brand new training school for nurses which had been founded by Dr Antoine Depage. Although often described as stern and aloof of by some of her young trainees, Edith was a natural teacher and gave the girls the very finest training and instilled great humane values in her aspiring nurses.

In July 1914 Edith was in Norfolk, dividing her time between her mother and family friends, the Harrisons at West Runton. When war was declared and the Germans on the

border of Belgium Edith was determined to return to Brussels. The clinique became a Red Cross Hospital. Edith impressed on the nurses that their first duty was to care for the wounded irrespective of nationality. She sent many of her nurses home but Edith, her chief assistant Elisabeth Wilkins, Sister Millicent White and a handful of others chose to remain, even after Brussels fell. Then, without discrimination they tended German soldiers as well as Belgians.

As the British retreated from Mons and the French were driven back, many from both armies ended up being stranded. In the Autumn of 1914, two bedraggled and wounded British soldiers, Colonel Dudley Boger and Sergeant Fred Meachin of 1st Battalion, The Cheshire Regiment found their way to the training school and were sheltered there for two weeks. More followed and soon an escape route to neutral territory in Holland was established. To Edith Cavell, as naive as it may seem to some sceptical modern historians, her motives were simple; the protection, concealment and the smuggling away of hunted men was as much a humanitarian act as the tending of the sick and wounded. Another soldier Pte Arthur Wood of 1st Battalion, The Norfolk Regiment recognised a print of Norwich Cathedral on the wall of her office, he lived on Quebec Road in the city; always delighted to receive someone from her beloved Norfolk, and recognising him as an intelligent and resourceful man with a good chance of making the escape asked him to take home her Bible and a letter for her Mother who was also then living in the city. By the time he was smuggled out, at the end of February 1915 an advanced escape route was established in conjunction with the Belgian underground, masterminded by the Prince and Princess de Croy. Guides were organised by Philippe Baucq and about 200 allied soldiers were helped to escape. All of those involved knew the risk they were taking – they could face a firing squad for harbouring allied soldiers. The secret escape organisation lasted for almost a year, until a Belgian collaborator passed through the Clinique and betrayed some members of the Belgian underground escape group. Edith knew it would not be long before they came for her. She was arrested on 5 August 1915, interrogated and imprisoned, mostly in solitary confinement, to await trial.

On Thursday 7 October 1915 thirty five members of the escape group were tried. The proceedings were conducted in German and translated into French. Edith Cavell wore her civilian clothes and gave her evidence in French. The hearing effectively lasted a day and the accused endured a weekend awaiting the sentence. Stoical and willing to confront the fate that almost certainly awaited her Edith read and found courage in the words of the bible. On Monday 11 October she learnt that the sentence of death had been passed on her (and four others) for 'conducting soldiers to the Enemy.'

A lurid depiction of the death of Nurse Cavell, from a contemporary postcard.

The trial and particularly the sentence had drawn international concern, diplomats discussed whether or not to intervene. Hugh Gibson, First Secretary of the American legation at Brussels, made clear to the German government that executing Cavell would further harm their nation's already damaged reputation, but no reprieve was granted; her execution was set for 12 October 1915 at the Tir Nationale (National Rifle Range). On the night before her execution German Lutheran Pastor Paul le Seur obtained permission for English Chaplain, Stirling Gahan, to visit her on the night before she died. His account of her last hours is very moving. They repeated the words of 'Abide with me', and Edith received the Sacrament. Edith then spoke with Gahan, she wished all he friends to know that she willingly gave her life for her country and said: 'I have seen death so often that it is not fearful or strange to me, and this I would say, standing as I do in view of God and Eternity. I realise patriotism is not enough. I must have no hatred or bitterness against anyone.'

Pastor le Seur accompanied Edith to her execution in the early morning hours of 12 October, his harrowing account was published in *The Truth* by Wilhelm Behrens:

'At the first grey of dawn, with a heavy heart, I got into the motor car and drove out to the prison. I sent in my name to Miss Cavell. If I remember rightly, the soldier told me she had just been kneeling at her table.

In the cell a flickering gas-flame was burning. Two large bouquets of withered flowers, which had been standing there for ten weeks, awakened the impression of a vault. The condemned lady had packed all her little property with the greatest care in a handbag.

I accompanied her through the long corridors of the great prison. The Belgian prison officials stood there and greeted her silently with the highest respect. She returned their greetings silently. Then we boarded the motor-car which awaited us in the yard...'

At the Tir Nationale a company at full war strength (two hundred and fifty men) stood there, in accordance with the regulations, under the command of a staff-officer. There were two poles a short distance from one another, the escape route guide Philippe Baucq was to be executed beside her.

Pastor le Seur continues: 'Then I led her a few steps to the pole, to which she was loosely bound. A bandage was put over her eyes, which, as the soldier who put it on told me, were full of tears. Then a few seconds passed, which appeared to me like eternity, because the Catholic clergyman spoke somewhat longer with M. Baucq, until he also stood at his pole. Immediately the sharp commands were given, two salvoes crashed at the same time — each of eight men at a distance of six paces — and the two condemned persons sank to the ground without a sound.'

Edith Cavell faced death with unflinching dignity and was buried in the sod of the firing range. There was international outcry to the 'Murder' of 'Nurse' Cavell (A forty nine year old Matron clearly did not have the same media appeal as the younger and pretty sounding 'Nurse') and the propaganda machine went

With white sheet draped over it, the crowd awaits Queen Alexandra to unveil the memorial to Edith Cavell on Tombland, 12 October 1918.

The vast crowd of thousands that crammed onto Tombland, Norwich to see the unveiling of the Cavell memorial 12 October 1918.

A close up view of the Cavell monument, a few days after it was unveiled.

Red Cross Nurse Christine Taylor was on parade at the unveiling of the Cavell memorial.

Final preparations on Edith Cavell's flag draped coffin on the gun carriage and escort for the final journey from Thorpe Station to Norwich Cathedral.

into full swing producing posters, papers, magazines, postcards, in memoriam cards and all sorts of paper souvenirs, some showing Edith's portrait, but far more artists impressions of the execution depicting an angelic nurse in full uniform, with the Red Cross emblazoned upon the breast of their apron facing the heathen German firing squad who would undoubtedly be using that international symbol of altruistic mercy and succour as a target; some even had a hulking German officer looming over her prostrate body with smoking revolver having delivered the coup de grace.

The country and our county did not (and does not) forget its greatest heroine of the First World War, a number of memorials were erected to her and on 12 October 1918 – three years to the day, the anniversary of her execution, thousands crammed into Tombland in Norwich to watch Queen Alexandra unveil the monument to Edith Cavell. Nurse Christine Taylor was one of the many Red Cross nurses who paraded for the occasion and recorded the event in a letter: 'were collected in the Cattle Market Drill Hall in our various detachments, men, nurses, band and all and after some manoeuvring were got into fours and marched out and put on Tombland as a guard along the side with some cadets and volunteers. The most amusing incident was when the sheet came off the statue of its own accord five minutes before the Queen was due. A little old man had to scramble up and just got it on again in time.'

After the armistice Edith's body was exhumed and returned to England to be given the honoured funeral she deserved. The Belgian Army guarded the coffin across Flanders to Ostend, where it was handed over to the Royal Navy. The destroyer *Rowena* carried it across the sea and Royal Navy ratings bore it ashore at Dover where it was taken through streets of mourners in a glass-sided hearse. In London the coffin was drawn on a gun carriage to Westminster Abbey and then after the service by train on its final journey to Norwich where, on 15 May 1919 the flag draped coffin was transported to the cathedral on a gun carriage. At the Erpingham Gate her coffin was taken onto the shoulders of six NCOs, a number of whom she had helped to escape. They solemnly carried her to her final resting place at Life's Green outside Norwich Cathedral where prayers were read, 'Abide with Me' sung and the Bishop pronounced the

blessing. The Last Post was then sounded and the *Nunc Dimittis* sung, and finally Edith Cavell, Christian, Patriot and Martyr was laid to rest in the soil of the county she was born into, knew and loved so well.

Tank!

It is a little known fact that when the tank was in development and a top secret new weapon of war they were put through their paces in a secret training area on Lord Iveagh's estate on the Norfolk and Suffolk borders at Elvedon near Thetford. To ensure no prying eyes could see long hoardings covered in hessian were put along the boundaries of the estate near public roads – the excuse being these were to protest passing traffic from gun shell explosions. When these landships were finally removed to the front line their secret was maintained by any reference in their shipment being referred to as 'tanks,' as in *water* tanks and the name stuck.

In the latter years of the war drives for War Savings and War Bonds to keep going the supply of weapons and equipment were held across the country, mostly in the guise of 'Tank Week.' The idea was that you bought the certificates or bonds, which would be used for the duration and then would be paid back 'eventually – with a high rate of interest'. Adverts were explicit and demanded the attention of every patriotic citizen; such as this one that appeared in the *Eastern Daily Press* on 25 March 1918:

Left: Senior Staff and Royal Engineer Officers, Norwich Tank Week 1918.

Right: Norwich Civic Dignitaries give an address to the crowd.

Almost £60,000 was raised by Thetford during their 'Tank Week.'.

'Every inhabitant of Norwich and District should buy National War Bonds or War Savings Certificates from the tank next week. You can buy a War Savings Certificate for 15/6 or a National War Bond for £5 or £5000 or any amount in between. Ask your friends to go with you to the tank. Go early and often. Beat every town in the Kingdom! It will be a matter of pride to you and your town.

Left: An enormous crowd gathers to watch the tank depart from Norwich.

Right: Great Yarmouth had a Submarine Week, but because the phenomena of the Tank was so thoroughly associated with War Savings the media referred to it as 'Tank Week' and they improvised their own – by cutting and fixing hoardings to a tram. Yarmouth raised £183,000.

It will be acclaimed by the men on the Sea and at the Front. It will be an historic week for your town.'

Norwich's Tank Week was held between Monday 1 and 6 April 1918. Each day the press covered the events, speeches and rallies around the tank and published a running total and notable donations. With a magnificent effort from the people of the city and help from sizable purchases of War Bonds by the City Corporation and Norwich Union Life Insurance Society, Norwich raised over a million pounds – the final figure being the phenomenal sum of £1,057,382.

8 The Armistice and After

One almighty cheer goes up from the Officers and Men of 51st and 52nd (Graduated) Battalion, The Bedfordshire Regiment on the announcement of the Armistice in Norwich Market Place on 11 November 1918.

The Armistice was announced at the eleventh hour of the eleventh day of the eleventh month 1918. Public announcements were made and impromptu celebrations were held across the county but no proper celebration could be held until 'the boys came home.' A date of 19 July 1919 was set for what was to be the national grand celebration of Peace Day.

On Peace Day in Norwich the bells of the churches rang out, a great Thanksgiving Service was held in the Cathedral followed by a procession to the Market Place where representative detachments from all the military and civilian forces in the county lined and filled a square and were given a fine address and tribute was given by the Lord Mayor. There were then great festivities, luncheons for returned servicemen and organised sports, fancy dress parades and special events held across the parks; it seemed like 'the whole of Norwich and his wife' turned out for the proceedings. Events mirroring these grand celebrations were held in every town and village across the county.

The writing is on the wall, the Armistice passed and the boys who had volunteered 'for the duration' just wanted to go home.

Tragically, the county was already counting the cost of the war. Thousands of families had lost loved ones but some still held out hope for their boy who had been posted 'missing' but as the weeks, months and years passed by after the Armistice they had to come to terms with the realisation that their son was never to return. Some mothers, wives and sweethearts never accepted it; many of those who did wore mourning black for the rest of their lives.

In 1920 the *Norfolk Roll of Honour* was published with returns from 626 of the 700

Norfolk parishes; it showed some 11,771 Norfolk men and women lost their lives in the war, over 2200 of them from Norwich. In its statistical summary it was estimated out of the total number of Norfolk people who served the proportion of them missing or killed was about 1 in 9. In the United Kingdom one man out of every 57 inhabitants was killed or reported missing. In Norfolk the proportion was even greater – one in 42. There were no casualties reported for the Parishes of Fishley, Stratton Strawless, Topcroft and Wheatacre.

The published figures could not include those who died in the ensuing years from wounds received or sickness contracted neither do they include the thousands of local men disabled in body, mind and soul during The Great War.

The genteel world of Victorian and Edwardian life and holidays in Norfolk had been shattered during the carnage of First World War, everybody lost somebody they knew, loved and cared for, soon there was talk of 'the loss of a generation.' Thousands of those young gentlemen had innocently walked arm-in-arm with their sweethearts and fiancées among the romantic fields of poppies across our county, along our coastal pathways, dotted and spread with the red flowers and lingered at the spiritual heartland of Poppyland, the Garden of Sleep at Sidestrand. Now many of them already lay dead on the fields of France and Flanders by 1916, when on 26 February 1916, as the plans for a 'Big Push' on the Somme were being formulated the church tower of the Garden of Sleep, the focal point and so emblematical of that magical world slipped, unwitnessed, over the edge of the cliff and was smashed to pieces on the beach below. On just the First Day of the Battle of the Somme on 1 July 1916 the British Army

A patriotic fancy dress costume parade at the Blakeney Peace Day Carnival 1919.

Bertie Withers, a private soldier from Norwich, severely wounded while serving with 4th Battalion, The Norfolk Regiment opens The Norwich War Memorial 8 October 1927. The fine memorial was designed by Sir Edwin Lutyens RA and was originally placed at the east end of the Guildhall.

The Market Place of Norwich filled by veterans and spectators at an Armistice Day in the late 1920s.

The unveiling ceremony of the East Dereham War Memorial by HRH Prince Henry on Sunday 22 October 1922.

Dedication of the East Harling War Memorial.

Unveiling of the Snettisham War Memorial.

Choirs and local people came from miles around to the dedication of the East Ruston War Memorial.

The unveiling of the Attleborough War Memorial June 24th 1920.

Norwich Street collectors for the first ever British Legion Earl Haig Fund Remembrance Day collection on 11 November 1921, some £106,000 was raised nationally for widows, orphans and the estimated 500,000 disabled British ex-servicemen.

Staff of the Norfolk County War Pensions Committee, November 1921. Their workload was a heavy one as thousands of Norfolk men returned home disabled and to find that there was not a 'land fit for heroes' awaiting them. Many men, because of their disabilities, could not return to their old jobs, some could never work again. Despite the best efforts of the committee staff many disabled soldiers endured great hardship in the 1920s and 30s.

One of the 'Honourably Discharged' of Norwich, his silver badge to denote this is worn on his lapel.

Tasburgh and District Branch of the British Legion on Armistice Day Parade 7 November 1926.

suffered over 57,000 casualties. Many had said in the years before that Poppyland would end when the tower fell. Like the tower, a generation fell and was never to be. The irony was not lost when poppies flowered 'between the crosses, row on row' in Flanders fields. Nothing was ever the same again.

We have now seen every Norfolk man and woman who served in the Great War pass away. Many of us can still remember them on Armistice Day parade, the one day a year most of them wore their medals and marched again with their old comrades. One of the last of them wrote: 'There can never be another war like the Great War, nor the comradeship and endurance we knew then. I think, perhaps, men are not like that now.'

Left: *Briston War Memorial. The loss of so many young men from rural communities made the sense of loss across the county all the more profound.*

Centre: *Holkham War Memorial erected by Thomas William, Third Earl of Leicester and Dedicated on 1 January 1920. The panels of the memorial list estate workers and young men from the village. One of the Earl's sons, Lt. the Hon. Arthur George Coke who died on 21 May 1915 while serving with No. 3 Squadron, Royal Naval Armoured Car Division, is named among the fallen.*

Right: *Scottow War Memorial on the day it was dedicated.*

Dedication of the Thetford War Memorial.

The men of Worstead who returned from their service in The First World War.

Appendix

The Distribution of Home Defence Troops in the County of Norfolk (1916)

Northern Army

Headquarters . . . . .Lynford Hall, Mundford

1st Cyclist Division . . . . .Bracondale, Norwich

6th Infantry Works Company . . . . .Pulham St Mary

3rd Cyclist Brigade Headquarters . . . . .Holt
2/1st Leicestershire Yeomanry
2/1st Staffordshire Yeomanry
2/1st Lincolnshire Yeomanry
Field Ambulance
Army Service Corps
Signal Troop
2/7th Welsh Cyclists (Attached)

4th Cyclist Brigade Headquarters . . . . .North Walsham
2/1st City of London Yeomanry . . . . .Westwick
2/1st County of London Yeomanry . . . . .Westwick
2/3rd County of London Yeomanry . . . . .Westwick
Field Ambulance . . . . .Westwick
Army Service Corps . . . . .North Walsham
Signal Troop . . . . .North Walsham
1/6th Norfolk Cyclists (Attached) . . . . .North Walsham

Divisional Army Service Corps . . . . .Norwich
Divisional Signal Company . . . . .Norwich
North Signal Company, Royal Engineers (Attached) . . . . .Norwich

64th (Highland) Division . . . . .Norwich

191st Brigade Headquarters . . . . .Kelling
2/4th Royal Highlanders
2/4th Seaforth Highlanders
2/6th Seaforth Highlanders
2/4th Cameron Highlanders

192nd Brigade Headquarters . . . . .Taverham
2/6th Royal Highlanders
2/7th Royal Highlanders
2/5th Gordon Highlanders
2/7th Gordon Highlanders

193rd Brigade Headquarters . . . . .Witton Park, North Walsham
2/6th Argyll and Sutherland Highlanders . . . . .Witton Park, North Walsham
2/7th Argyll and Sutherland Highlanders . . . . .Bacton
2/8th Argyll and Sutherland Highlanders. . . . . .Witton Park, North Walsham
2/9th Argyll and Sutherland Highlanders . . . . .Witton Park, North Walsham

3rd Provincial Brigade
Headquarters . . . . .Holt
43rd Provisional Battalion . . . . .Weybourne
62nd Provisional Battalion . . . . .Sheringham
64th Provisional Battalion . . . . .Salthouse
67th Provisional Battalion . . . . .Cley
3rd Provisional Battery, Royal Field Artillery .Salthouse
Ammunition Column . . . . .Bodham
Field Company Royal Engineers . . . . .Weybourne
Brigade Field Ambulance . . . . .Letheringsett
Brigade Army Service Corps . . . . .Holt
2/1st Fife Heavy Battery, Royal Garrison Artillery . . . . .Sheringham

4th Provincial Brigade
Headquarters . . . . .North Walsham
46th Provisional Battalion . . . . .Happisburgh
47th Provisional Battalion . . . . .Mundesley
48th Provisional Battalion . . . . .Cromer
49th Provisional Battalion . . . . .Hemsby
4th Provisional Battery, Royal Field Artillery . . . . .Catfield
Ammunition Column . . . . .Catfield
No. 2 Armoured Train . . . . .North Walsham
Field Company Royal Engineers . . . . .Great Ormesby
Brigade Field Ambulance . . . . .Wroxham
Brigade Army Service Corps . . . . .Wroxham
2/1st (Home Counties), Kent Heavy Battery
Royal Garrison Artillery . . . . .Mundesley

5th Provincial Brigade
Headquarters . . . . .St Olaves

Above right: The bands of 2/6th and 2/7th Battalions of The Black Watch (foreground) and 2/5th and 2/7th Gordon Highlanders on parade on Mousehold Heath, June 1916.

Above left: Gordon Highlander Pipes and Drums Norwich, 1916.

63rd Provisional Battalion . . . . .Great Yarmouth
65th Provisional Battalion . . . .Great Yarmouth
68th Provisional Battalion . . . . .Pakefield
69th Provisional Battalion . . . . .Lowestoft
5th Provisional Battery, Royal Field Artillery . . . . .Great Yarmouth
Ammunition Column . . . . .Great Yarmouth
Field Company Royal Engineers . . . . .Pakfield
Brigade Field Ambulance . . . . .Oulton Broad
Brigade Army Service Corps . . . . .St Olaves
2/1st (Essex) Heavy Battery
Royal Garrison Artillery . . . . .Lowestoft

Divisional Troops

Divisional Cavalry and Cyclists . . . . .Taverham
'C' Squadron, 2/1st Glasgow Yeomanry
Divisional Cyclist Company

Artillery Headquarters . . . . .Norwich
320th Brigade Field Artillery . . . . .Blickling
'A' Battery, 293rd Brigade (Attached) . . . . .Blickling
321st Brigade Field Artillery . . . . .Worstead
'B' Battery, 293rd Brigade (Attached) . . . . .Worstead
'A' Echelon, Divisional Ammunition Column . . . . .Rackheath Park

The Highlanders' March to Cromer.

Hark to the pibroch, the pipes and the drum ?
It's the Highlanders playing a march as they come.
Scotland's brave sons from the heather-tipped Bens,
" The flowers O' the forest " from mountains and glens.

The Black Watch march first, at the front may be seen
In their dark tartan kilts of the blue and the green.
Though the best have been killed by the Huns o'er the sea,
" We'll up with the bonnets O' bonnie Dundee."

The Chief of the Seaforth's, MacKenzie the head,
In kilts of dark blue and green, white stripes and red,
To Sheringham march, the Argyles there to greet,
With the Campbells are coming they play through the street

The third in the march are the Cameron men,
Locheil, is their chief, but he's no from Cockpen.
Their bonnie bright tartan of yellows and reds,
The lassies O' Cromer are clean off their heads.

" The Cock O' the North," the pipers do play,
In Royal Stuart kilts of that clan once so gay.
A famous red tartan so brilliant and braw,
As when Bonnie Prince Charlie was Heid O' them a".

When these Highland laddies from Cromer depart,
Their bonnie wee lassies must cheer up each heart,
" If when fighting the Huns, ye are wounded and sad,
Then "whistle and I'll come to ye my lad."

"THISTLE,"
BRACONDALE,
M. MACKAY GREEN.   CROMER.

Engineers Headquarters . . . . .Norwich
2/1st Highland Field Company . . . . .Taverham
3/2nd Highland Field Company . . . . .Witton Park
1/3rd Highland Field Company . . . . .Kelling
Divisional Signal Company . . . . .Norwich

Army Service Corps
533rd Headquarter Company . . . . .Norwich
534th Company . . . . .Worstead
535th Company . . . . .Taverham
536th Company . . . . .Kelling
52nd Field Butchery . . . . .Norwich
57th Field Bakery . . . . .Norwich
278th Depot Unit of Supply .Taverham
309th Depot Unit of Supply . . . . .Kelling
310th Depot Unit of Supply . . . . .Norwich
349th Depot Unit of Supply . . . . .Honing

Royal Army Medical Corps
Headquarters . . . . .Norwich
3/1st Highland Field Ambulance . . . . .Edingthorpe
2/2nd Highland Field Ambulance . . . . .Kelling
2/3rd Highland Field Ambulance . . . . .Taverham
Divisional Sanitary Section . . . . .Norwich
Divisional Casualty Clearing Station . . . . .Norwich

Mobile Veterinary Section . . . . .Costessey

Select Bibliography

Christopher Andrew, *Secret Service: The Making of the British Intelligence Community* (London 1985)

G. Balfour, *The Armoured Train; It Development and Usage* (London 1981)

Jeremy Bastin, *The Norfolk Yeomanry in Peace and War* (Fakenham 1986)

Christopher Bird, *Silent Sentinels* (Dereham 1999)

J.P. Blake (ed.) *The Official Regulations for Volunteer Training Corps and for County Volunteer Organisations (England and Wales)* (London 1916)

Thekla Bowser, *The Story of British VAD Work in the Great War,* (London 1925)

John Canning, *1914* (London 1967)

James Cantlie, *First Aid to the Injured* (London 1910)

James Cantlie, *Red Cross Training Manual No.3* (London 1914)

Tim Carew, *The Royal Norfolk Regiment* (London 1967)

H G Castle, *Fire Over England* (London 1982)

Randolph Churchill, *Twenty-One Years* (London 1964)

Winston S.Churchill, *His Father's Son: The Life of Randolph Churchill* (London 1996)

A. E. Clark-Kennedy, *Edith Cavell: Pioneer and Patriot* (London 1965)

Terry Davy, *Dereham in the Great War* (Dereham 1990)

A. Campbell Erroll, *A History of Sheringham and Beeston Regis* (Sheringham 1970)

Val Fiddian (ed.), *Salthouse: The Story of a Norfolk Village* (Salthouse 2003)

Helen Fraser, *Women and War Work* (New York 1918)

Harold Hood, *Illustrated Memorial of the East Coast Raids by the German Navy and Airships* (Middlesborough 1915)

C. B. Hawkins, *Norwich: A Social Study* (London 1910)

Lt Col Ronnie Cole Mackintosh, *A Century of Service to Mankind* (London 1994)

L L Gore, *The History of Hunstanton* (Bognor Regis 1983)

Gerald Gliddon (ed.), *Norfolk & Suffolk in the Great War* (Norwich 1988)

Jane Hales, *A Tale of the Norfolk Red Cross* Watton 1970

Holcombe Ingleby, *The Zeppelin Raid in West Norfolk* (London 1915)

Brigadier E A James, *British Regiments 1914-18* (fourth edition) (London 1993)

Tom Jerrold, *Our War-Time Kitchen Garden* (London 1917)

Major J H Kennedy, *Attleborough in War Time* (London c1920)

Peter Kent, *Fortifications of East Anglia* (Lavenham 1988)

P.S. King, *The Volunteer Force and the Volunteer Training Corps during the Great War: Official Record of the Central Association Volunteer Regiments –* (London 1920)

Colonel C E Knight MBE, *The Auxiliary Hospitals The British Red Cross Society and St John Ambulance in Norfolk 1914-1919* (Norwich 1989)

Herbert Leeds (ed.) *Norwich Peace Souvenir* (Norwich 1920)

Dan McCaffery, *Air Aces: The Lives and Times of Twelve Canadian Fighter Pilots* (Toronto, Canada 1990)

Lyn MacDonald, *1914* (London 1987)

Arthur Mee, *The King's England: Norfolk* (London 1940)

Captain Joseph Morris, *The German Air Raids on Great Britain* (London 1969)

Maurice Morson, *A Force Remembered* (Derby 2000)

H. Newhouse (Recruiting Officer), *A Little Chat about The 1st (City of Norwich) Battalion, Norfolk Volunteers* (Norwich 1916)

Bob Ogley, Mark Davison, Ian Currie, *The Norfolk and Suffolk Weather Book* (Westerham 1993)

Peter Parker, *The Old Lie* (London 1987)

F. Loraine Petre, *The History of the Norfolk Regiment* vol.II (Norwich 1924)

Dr Eric Puddy, *A History of the Order of St John of Jerusalem in Norfolk* (Dereham 1961)

W J Reader, *At Duty's Call: A Study in Obsolete Patriotism* (Manchester 1988)

A V Sellwood, *The Saturday Night Soldiers* (London 1966)

W. E. Shewell-Cooper, *Land Girl: A Manual for Volunteers in the Women's Land Army* (London 1941)

Sue Smart, *When Heroes Die* (Derby 2001)

Jonathan Riley-Smith, *Hospitallers: The History of The Order of St John* (London 1999)

Rowland Ryder, *Edith Cavell* (London 1975)

C.F. Snowden Gamble, *The Story of a North Sea Air Station* (London 1928)

Neil Storey, *A Century of Norwich* (Stroud 2000)

Neil Storey, *A Norfolk Century* (Stroud 1999)

Neil Storey, *Norfolk at War* (Stroud 1995)

Neil Storey, *The Royal Norfolk Regiment* (Stroud 1997)

Warner, Philip *Field-Marshal Earl Haig* (London 1991)

A Rawlinson, *The Defence of London 1915-18* (London 1923)

Peter M. Walker, *Norfolk Military Airfields* (Norwich 1997)

Ray Westlake, *The Territorial Battalions* (London 1986)

Ray Westlake, *British Battalions in France & Belgium 1914* (Barnsley 1997)

Henry Wills, *Pillboxes* (Leo Cooper 1985)

Emily Wood, *The Red Cross* (London 1995)

R J Wyatt, *Death from the Skies* (Norwich 1990)

Reference Books and Government Publications

Kelly's Directory of Cambridgeshire, Norfolk and Suffolk (London 1912)

A Pictorial and Descriptive Record of the Red Cross Hospitals of Norwich and Norfolk (Norwich 1917)

St John Ambulance Association, *Annals of the Ambulance Department* (London 1929)

Norfolk News Company, *Norfolk Roll of Honour 1914 - 18* (Norwich 1920)

City of Norwich, Public Library Committee,*Norwich Roll of Honour 1914-19* (Norwich 1920)

War Office, *Scheme for the Organisation of Voluntary Aid in England and Wales* (HMSO 1909)

War Office, *Scheme for the Organisation of Voluntary Aid in England and Wales* (December 1910 Revision) (HMSO 1910)

Reports

British Red Cross Society & Order of St John of Jerusalem, *Financial Statement of The Joint War Committee* (London 1918)

British Red Cross Society & Order of St John of Jerusalem, *Final Reports by the Joint War Committee and the Joint War Finance Committee of the British Red Cross Society and Order of St John of Jerusalem in England on Voluntary Aid Rendered to the Sick and Wounded at Home and Abroad and to British Prisoners of War 1914-19* (HMSO 1921)

British Red Cross Society *Norfolk Branch Report 1918* (Norwich 1919)

Britsh Red Cross Society *Norfolk Branch Report 1919* (Norwich 1920)

St John Ambulance, *X District Reports* 1909 – 1919

Newspapers & Journals

Aeroplane Monthly
First Aid, Journal of The St John Ambulance Brigade
The Red Cross, Journal of The British Red Cross Society
Carrow Works Magazine
Dereham & Fakenham Times
East Anglian Daily Times
Eastern Daily Press
Lynn News
Norfolk Fair
Norfolk Chronicle
Norwich Mercury
The War Illustrated
The Volunteer Training Corps Gazette
The Times
The Daily Express
The Daily Mirror
Punch Magazine
Yarmouth Mercury

Sources

National Archives

WO 33/779 Distribution of Home Defence Troops (1916)

WO 33/828 Approved armaments and Anti-Aircraft guns (1917)

WO 339/46 Service papers of Lieut Cyril Loftus Stocker, Norfolk Regiment

WO 339/25422 Service papers of Lieut T A Buckland, Norfolk Regiment

WO 372 Service Medal and Award Rolls Index, First World War

WO 372/23 Women's Services, Distinguished Conduct Medals and Military Medals

AIR 1/2123/207/73/2 Intelligence Section report on enemy airship raids on Britain (January-June 1915)

AIR 1/2123/207/73/3 Intelligence Section report on enemy airship raids on Britain (August-September 1915)

AIR 1/2123/207/73/12 Intelligence Section report on enemy airship raids on Britain (September-October 1916)

AIR 1/2123/207/73/28 Intelligence Section report on enemy airship raids on Britain on enemy airship raids on Britain (June-August 1918)

Norfolk Record Office,

For Smith-Dorrien's General Line of evacuation of the civil population see:
NRO, MC 947/1

Deposit made by Colonel C E Knight MBE: Material relating to Voluntary Aid Societies: St John Ambulance Brigade and British Red Cross Society
NRO, SO161/1-37

Internet Sources

Commonwealth War Graves Commission
www.cwgc.org/debt_of_honour.asp

Royal Navy Submarine Museum
www.rnsubmus.co.uk
(Submarine Losses 1904 To Present Day)

The Aerodrome: Aces and Aircraft of World War One
www.theaerodrome.com

The Story of Edith Cavell
www.edithcavell.org.uk

U Boat Net (German OB 3/11/14 and loss of Yorck)
www.uboat.net